The
THIRTIES

A Reconsideration
in the Light of
the American
Political Tradition

The THIRTIES

New Foreword by Charles R. Kesler

MORTON J. FRISCH, Editor

MARTIN DIAMOND, Editor

IRVING KRISTOL

HOWARD ZINN

LESLIE A. FIEDLER

FRANK KNIGHT

ORME W. PHELPS

RAYMOND MOLEY

REXFORD G. TUGWELL

ERNEST K. LINDLEY

UPTON SINCLAIR

NORTHERN ILLINOIS UNIVERSITY PRESS DeKalb

© 2010 by Northern Illinois University Press

Published by the Northern Illinois University Press, DeKalb, Illinois 60115

Manufactured in the United States using postconsumer-recycled, acid-free paper.

All Rights Reserved

ISBN: 978-0-87580-632-7

The Library of Congress has cataloged the hardcover edition as follows:

The thirties: a reconsideration in the light of the American political tradition

   p.

1. Nineteen thirties. 2. United States—History—1933–1945. I. Frisch,

Morton J., ed. II. Diamond, Martin, 1919– ed.

E806.S46 1966   67026266

Acknowledgment: The author wishes to thank City Lights Books for

permission to reprint lines from HOWL AND OTHER POEMS

by Allen Ginsberg, © 1959 by Allen Ginsberg.

Contents

Foreword

IN 1966, CLAREMONT MEN'S COLLEGE (CMC) held a conference on the Great Depression and the New Deal. Two years later, a slender volume of conference proceedings appeared: *The Thirties: A Reconsideration in the Light of the American Political Tradition*. When the Northern Illinois University Press invited me to write a Foreword to its republication of *The Thirties*, I agreed at once, because this book, long out of print, is a forgotten gem among studies of the period and sheds light on our own renewed debate over government stimulus of the economy, the future of the American welfare state, how (or whether!) to interpret the Constitution, the relation between political moderation and extremism, and the proper size and scope of the federal government.

Very much on the conference participants' minds were the cultural and political upheavals of the 1960s. In a broad sense, the book looks at the Thirties from the perspective of the Sixties, trying to understand the causes and consequences of these periods of social and political change, and to discern their similarities and differences. Today, in the midst of a milder but still audacious attempt to remake the national government's authority over health care, financial markets, and energy and environmental regulation, we are interested to see what we can learn from the New Deal, and from our authors' efforts to come to terms with it in the Sixties. They had all lived through it one way or another, most as then-obscure young men, a few as conspicuous players on the stage of events. But the conference's theme prompted almost all of them to connect their autobiographical observations to the American political tradition, and to measure their experience of the 1930s against the political assumptions of the '20s and before, as well as against the ideas circulating in the 1960s.

They had an apt venue for these inquiries. Claremont Men's College (it went co-ed in the 1970s and became Claremont McKenna College) had been founded in 1946, in the shadow of World War II, and with a focus on "political economy" that reflected the continuing influence of the Depression and the New Deal. Economics and Political Science were its flagship departments, boasting as many faculty members and twice as many concentrators as the College's other departments combined. The founding president, George C.S. Benson, was a Harvard Ph.D. in political science and public administration but, despite that pedigree, was not a New Deal enthusiast. As can be teased out from his introductory statement in the book, when it came to the New Deal, he was ready to admit its good intentions but quick to question its excesses. Benson helped to ensure that the faculty in the two core departments contained both supporters and skeptics of the Thirties' innovations, so that CMC on the whole reflected his doubts about the changes in American political economy. Compared to the rest of the American professoriate, however, CMC seemed defiantly conservative on the subject, an impression that Benson was happy not to dispel. At any rate, impatient with the New Deal's simple glorification (see Arthur M. Schlesinger, Jr.'s, starry-eyed *The Age of Roosevelt*), the faculty, administration, and students of the College were prepared to entertain an unusually wide range of interpretations of "that tumultuous decade," as Benson called it.

The American Political Tradition Seminars, as they were titled formally, had been organized by Martin Diamond, a student of Leo Strauss's and an expert on *The Federalist* who had joined the CMC Political Science department in 1955. A socialist in his youth, he renounced that creed and made his scholarly reputation by defending the Constitution's democratic credentials against their quasi-Marxist denigration by Charles Beard and other Progressives. Diamond was a great teacher—one of the best of his generation—and he had great connections, which he drew upon to assemble the remarkable list of participants in the year's program. They ranged from the Pulitzer Prize-winning novelist and ardent socialist (and 1934 Democratic candidate for governor of California) Upton Sinclair to the man who would soon be hailed as the godfather of neoconservatism, Irving Kristol. Included were two key members of FDR's "brains trust," Raymond Moley and Rexford G. Tugwell, as well as Roosevelt's first biographer and sometime speechwriter, Ernest K. Lindley. On the economic side, Diamond called on Frank Knight, a founder of the Chicago School of free-market economics that would transform the field in the second half of the twentieth century, and Orme W. Phelps, a CMC economist sympathetic to the American labor movement. Leslie A. Fiedler, a well-known literary critic and man of the Left, and Howard Zinn, then an antiwar historian and activist (who later became famous as the author of *A People's History of the United States*, the bestselling radical account of the American past), were enlisted, too. Rounding out the contributors is Diamond's friend and co-editor, Morton J. Frisch. Another student of Leo Strauss's, Frisch was a decorated veteran of the Second World War (in addition to American medals, he received the Belgian Croix de Guerre for his heroism in the Battle of the Bulge) who had recently joined Northern Illinois University to help start its program in political philosophy. A beloved teacher, Frisch's scholarly interests ran to American political thought and particularly to Alexander Hamilton and Franklin Roosevelt; he would later write a book on each.

The reader of *The Thirties* will soon discover the charms of the contributors and can weigh the strengths and weaknesses of each chapter. The editors did not change the "informality," as they call it, of the contributions, which were originally presented orally. As anyone who spends time on campuses or watching CSPAN knows, most oral presentations are not worth the paper they're printed on. Happily, in this case, the speakers' remarks were not only interesting but unusually polished—Kristol's, indeed, are lapidary. The few chapters that are more colloquial, especially Leslie Fiedler's and Upton Sinclair's, have compensating advantages. In a class by itself is the conversation among the old Roosevelt hands: Moley, Tugwell, and Lindley. It is informative and richly revealing, and one wishes it had gone on longer. A few errors of transcription crept into the book, which due to technical limitations could not be corrected in this republication. The most amusing occurs in Fiedler's piece, which consistently mentions "pop," as in soda, where plainly he said "pot," as in marijuana.

The Thirties has less to say about the causes of the Great Depression than one might like. Knight discusses them in passing, for his real subject is the multitudinous economic and political measures of the

New Deal and their premises. John Maynard Keynes is mentioned frequently in the volume, and many economists and historians, including
Schlesinger, have made much of his influence on the New Deal's ulti-
mate understanding of the Depression's cause and cure. But as Tugwell
and Moley make clear, Keynes had no substantial influence on the formulation of New Deal policies. His great treatise, *The General Theory of
Employment, Interest, and Money*, did not appear until 1936; and when
he called on the President in 1934, Roosevelt was unimpressed. That
"damned Englishman is trying to tell us what we're doing already," FDR
complained to Tugwell. But implicit in our authors' passing references
to Keynes is the prestige his explanation of the Depression enjoyed
from the 1940s through the 1960s. In those decades, Keynesianism
enjoyed a bull market in textbook sales and academic hires, becoming
an orthodoxy so pervasive that even President Richard Nixon admitted, in 1971, that he too was a believer. Although he never actually said
"We are all Keynesians now," he might as well have.

According to Keynesian theory, the maldistribution of income in
the 1920s resulted in the well-to-do pouring their extra savings into the
stock market; the rich were *so* rich they could not spend it all on still
more houses and durable goods. When the overvalued stock market
collapsed, factories shut down and millions of people lost their jobs,
consumer spending dropped, and businesses stopped investing. The
poor and middle classes, who needed the durable goods and houses,
could not afford them. What caused the Depression, in the short run,
was thus under-consumption or "insufficient aggregate demand," as
the Keynesians called it, which could be cured by the government's
pumping up aggregate demand through deficit-financed spending. To
take care of the underlying, long-term problem of economic inequality, government would get into the business of redistributing income
from those with too much to those with too little, righting, in one
stroke, moral as well as economic wrong.

This argument still commanded the heights at the time *The Thirties*
was published. But its authority eroded considerably after the stag-
flation of the 1970s proved immune to Keynesian therapies. In the
meantime, the intellectual groundwork for a new economic diagno-
sis of the Depression and a new set of economic prescriptions had

been laid in the work of the Chicago School. Milton Friedman and Anna Schwartz's *A Monetary History of the United States*, published in 1963 and alluded to in Knight's chapter, blamed the Depression and the bank collapses of 1932-33 on massive policy mistakes by the Federal Reserve, which effectively contracted the money supply precisely when it should have expanded it. Friedman, who won the Nobel Prize in Economics in 1976, doubted, too, in his so-called "permanent income hypothesis," that temporary increases in personal income would result in the large increases in consumption counted on by Keynesian-style fiscal stimulus policies. Along the same lines, economists took aim at the perverse consequences of Herbert Hoover's and Franklin Roosevelt's efforts (via the Smoot-Hawley Tariff and the National Industrial Recovery Act, for example) to prop up wage rates as a means of boosting aggregate demand. Nor have the supply-side effects of the New Deal escaped criticism. In the past decade or so, scholars and popular writers alike have argued that FDR's tax increases—by 1936 the highest marginal federal income tax rate was 79 percent—combined with his denunciations of businessmen, empowerment of unions, and increases in government regulation prolonged the Depression by discouraging capitalists from investing and entrepreneurs from starting new businesses.

After the financial meltdown of 2008-9, Keynesian economics enjoyed a revival, and President Barack Obama's administration enacted a large stimulus bill, even as the Federal Reserve, headed by Ben Bernanke, an expert on the Great Depression, strove to avoid the Fed.'s past errors by vastly expanding the money supply and taking creative steps to increase the flow of credit to banks and businesses. Still, the reader should know that the mid-twentieth century view that maldistribution of income and under-consumption were the causes of the Depression and that fiscal stimulus and redistributive policies were its cure has retreated considerably. As skepticism toward that view has increased, so has the prominence of a new account that regards the Depression not as the crisis of capitalism but as a tragic example of a business downturn deepened, prolonged, and exploited by misbegotten government policies.

Where *The Thirties* shines, however, is in its treatment of the culture and especially the politics of the period in the light of America's changing, and unchanging, political ideas. Here three short observations may be of assistance:

First, the book provides some fascinating insights into the American Left. Phelps attends to the mainstream unions and their efforts to organize and gain federal protection for a right to organize. Fiedler and Zinn are doubtless supportive of that goal but operate, so to speak, in a different universe. They focus on the harder cultural and political Left—the Old Left that was Communist or Communist-inspired. As a literary critic, Fiedler brings to life the scorn that the literary Left of the 1930s felt for the New Deal and for all efforts to temporize or compromise rather than advance the Revolution that would, somehow or other, redeem life and literature by utterly transforming capitalist America. Among other things, he resurrects, strikingly, Alger Hiss's personal contempt for FDR as the paralyzed president of a paralyzed nation. And Fiedler shows how much the 1960s' divisions between leftist intellectuals and the American middle class (so fatal to liberalism's hopes ever since) had their origins in the 1930s, when almost all the best writers were Red. Of course, the irony is that the '30s led not to the Revolution but to the Affluent Society, a nightmare from which Fiedler was still trying to wake up.

Zinn offers an illuminating comparison of the Old Left and the New. He had studied the former and was a member, or at least a supporter, of the latter. His account remains instructive for our own times, as we gaze back on both the Sixties and the Thirties. As he notes, the Old Left was highly ideological and frankly committed to a nation and a system: to the Soviet Union and socialism. Radicals in the '30s were forever organizing and preparing, paradoxically, for the Revolution whose advent was historically determined and whose results were historically guaranteed. By contrast, the young radicals of the 1960s were suspicious of organization, political parties, historical inevitability, heroic leaders, and bureaucratic discipline. Overwhelmingly a student movement, the New Left was "existentialist," according to Zinn, meaning distrustful of reason and expertise; it wanted to do its own thing, to free its adherents up to follow and even to create their own authentic selves. "Love alone is radical," as a young woman in the Student Non-violent Coordinating Committee (SNCC) put it. Love alone is also lawless. Thus Sixties' radicalism was not always nonviolent, despite the peaceful example of the civil rights movement, whose influence radiated throughout the Left and well beyond.

It is safe to say that twenty-first century American liberalism is still struggling to reconcile the New Deal's idea of progress, of a moral direction or even inevitability in history, with the New Left's notion of radical autonomy and self-creation.

Second, *The Thirties* sheds light on the puzzle of Franklin Delano Roosevelt. His character and, by extension, the character of the whole New Deal, continue to mystify historians. Was he an ideologue masquerading as a pragmatist? a pragmatist masquerading as an ideologue? or something else again? Did he come to save capitalism, or to bury it? Quite sensibly, the reader finds here suggestions that the polarity of pragmatist and ideologue does not capture all the possibilities and that the quality of FDR's ideas ought to be examined more closely. Disagreements remain, but they are fruitful disagreements among our authors. Moley and Tugwell, who worked for him, seem more concerned with the "struggle for Roosevelt's mind" than with its native contents, but perhaps that is the adviser's occupational bias. Zinn and Fiedler are not interested in nonradical ideas. Knight doubts that FDR had, properly speaking, any economic ideas, and considers his political ideas presumptuous and, when backed as they were, for a while, by all the force of plebiscitary democracy, dangerous.

Kristol distinguishes between FDR's mind and the New Deal's. The latter represented a confluence of three liberal schools of thought, he argues—Keynesianism; the individualist progressivism of Louis Brandeis, Felix Frankfurter, and Woodrow Wilson; and the centralized regulatory and planning progressivism of Theodore Roosevelt, Herbert Croly, and such Brains Trusters as Tugwell. But Kristol avers that FDR's "great accomplishment" was not to take too seriously "any of the unemployed ideas that were then drifting idly through the country." In his own mind Roosevelt was a pragmatist, according to Kristol, thus fitting "Walter Bagehot's definition of the constitutional statesman: 'a nature at once active and facile . . . a large placid adaptive intellect." In this essay, Kristol's most considered statement on the 1930s and never before republished or collected elsewhere, he concludes that "FDR's genius—and I use the term advisedly—was his ability to inspire in the American people the confidence that all his programs . . . were simply extensions of the philosophy of the founding fathers." In short, Roosevelt "rooted American liberalism in a deeper American conservatism. . . ."

"Ten Years in a Tunnel" deserves to be considered a classic statement of the neoconservative defense of FDR and the New Deal. It displays as well some of the surprising points of sympathy between Kristol's views of capitalism and the American character, and those of Herbert Croly, whom Kristol quotes at a crucial juncture. He agrees with Croly, for example, that the choice between "the promise of American life" (understood as a constantly rising standard of living resulting from the individual pursuit of self-interest) and a "purpose" for American life (defined politically and authoritatively for citizens as such) is "the central issue" of modern American politics. At the same time, the essay contains a lucid critique of the New Deal's moral and political limitations, as bequeathed to later generations in the form of an amoral politics of interest groups and group rights.

Yet in contrast to Kristol's depreciation of the role of principles or ideology in FDR's statesmanship, Lindley emphasizes how steeped Roosevelt was in the ideas of the Progressive movement, along both its TR and Wilson lines. Long before the Depression and the Brains Trust came along, FDR's political vision had been set. From a different standpoint, Frisch comes to a similar and even stronger conclusion. Although FDR did not know "the deepest roots of . . . his political actions," he "did act, and did know, *in principle*, the character of the change his actions were bringing about." FDR meant to expand the older American liberalism, argues Frisch, to include not merely protection for the pursuit of happiness or for the conditions of happiness, but for happiness itself, understood primarily as "well-being" or "welfare." This new goal for American political life was manifested in the New Deal's elevation of "economic rights" to the quasi-constitutional status of a "second Bill of Rights." For Frisch, in other words, FDR was a conscious founder or refounder of an American way of life, of the American regime.

Third, and finally, I should mention what may strike many readers as the book's most curious omission: that it says very little about anti-New Deal conservatism. As significant as Kristol's defense of Roosevelt and neoconservatism's embrace of the New Deal were, these represented minority positions within the modern American conservative movement. William F. Buckley, Jr., Barry Goldwater, and Ronald Reagan made no secret of their opposition to the welfare and administrative state that the New Deal had begotten. Even though in Reagan's case he had voted for FDR four times, he came to see that the philosophy of the New Deal was, so he liked to say, really a form of fascism. He was probably thinking of the National Industrial Recovery Act, widely condemned as fascist in its own day. When the Supreme Court struck down the NIRA, it did Roosevelt a favor, helping to moderate the New Deal despite itself. The failure of FDR's "court packing" plan worked a similar effect. The New Deal that Kristol and Frisch praise was a more moderate and liberal one than it might have been had it gone unchecked at several turns by appeals to the letter and spirit of the Constitution. Knight, Moley, and Tugwell, each in his own way, make a correlative point: the New Deal's career of reform came to an end well before the beginning of World War II because its measures were becoming unpopular, and FDR had the political sense to recognize this.

Conservatism since the 1960s has not abandoned its objections to the New Deal, even though it has learned to live, somewhat uneasily, with the welfare state. That unease stems from the fact that the reasons adduced for a modest welfare state can easily be cited in justification of a Swedish one. And the growth over time of the federal government's budget, entitlement promises, and bureaucratic ambitions threatens to reopen the fundamental questions raised but never quite settled by the New Deal—questions concerning the nature and limits of republican government. *The Thirties* does not solve these questions, but it does put them into the right context: the principles of the American political tradition.

Charles R. Kesler
Claremont McKenna College
2010

Introductory Letter

Looking back on the 1930's today, I still remember it as an exciting time. Franklin Delano Roosevelt became President in March, 1933. Within one hundred days Congress, at his behest, had passed a mass of legislation which could have substantially altered the face of the economy. Some of it is still in effect. Looking back on the one hundred days, Garet Garrett wrote "The revolution was," and contended that the constitutional system and the whole political and economic temper of the country had been irrevocably changed by the early days of the New Deal.

There were substantial changes. Defenders say that it was in the American tradition; that what was done had to be done to keep the country from revolution and ruin. Was it a break with American tradition, or was it simply an adaptation within the purpose of the Constitution? It probably was some of both. Whatever it was, there is no doubt that the early New Deal and, in fact, the whole decade of the Thirties set a pattern which has had a vast effect on American political and economic life. Many of the ideas that were planted then have come to fruition in the Sixties under the present administration.

Today is far different from the Thirties, so far as technology and economic life are concerned. But the basic ideological questions remain the same and the parallels between the Sixties and the Thirties, as they relate to government, are remarkable. We today (particularly college students, to whom the Thirties are now ancient history) cannot ignore these similarities, if we are to understand the world in which we live.

What can we learn from that tumultuous decade of the 1930's? What must we do to preserve the free institutions we prize so highly? A review of those hectic days of the New Deal can shed much light for us if we have eyes to see.

GEORGE C. S. BENSON
PRESIDENT, CLAREMONT MEN'S COLLEGE
1968

Preface

THESE ESSAYS were originally presented as lectures at the annual Seminars on the American Political Tradition which took place at Claremont Men's College on February 22, 23, and 24, 1966.

The American Political Tradition Seminars consist of a series of lectures, forums, and related events designed to examine important periods and problems in American life in the light of the American political tradition. The central feature of the seminars is its adaptation for undergraduates of the format used by professional scholarly societies. Formal papers are presented for criticism to a panel of professional colleagues and student participants. The seminars explore the annual theme in a number of other ways which make for an intensive three days: an opening address; an appropriate debate or symposium involving major public figures; dramatic readings by a distinguished actor; plays and motion pictures relating to the year's theme; historical exhibits; and many activities designed to draw together Claremont students and visiting scholars.

The following papers were written to be presented orally, and accordingly, many of them will display a kind of informality not always characteristic of essays which appear in learned journals. However, we do not believe that their informality detracts from their scholarly character. In fact, the editors sought to preserve as much of that informality as possible.

The discussants of the papers presented at the seminars were Professor Douglass G. Adair, Claremont Graduate School; Professor Irving Bernstein; UCLA; Professor Langdon Elsbree, Claremont Men's College; Mr. Daniel Fuchs, Beverly Hills,

California; Professor Harry V. Jaffa, Claremont Men's College; Professor Alan Lawson, University of California at Irvine; Professor Robert Meyners, Claremont Men's College; Professor Robert A. Nisbet, University of California at Riverside; Professor Melvin W. Reder, Stanford University; Professor David S. Sanders, Harvey Mudd College; Mr. William French Smith, Los Angeles, California; Professor Paul E. Sultan, Claremont Graduate School; Professor Procter Thomson, Claremont Men's College; and Professor Daniel C. Vandermeulen, Claremont Graduate School. The student discussants were Messrs. John Edwards, David Fawcett, Aaron Fuller, Joseph Malkin and David Reid. Mr. Richard Zinman acted as special assistant in connection with the Thirties program.

We wish to thank Mrs. Joseph Brophy and Mrs. Morton Frisch who generously undertook the difficult task of taking manuscripts from the tapes, and would like to express our gratitude to Claremont Men's College for permission to publish these seminars as well as to the individual contributors who presented papers. We owe a special word of thanks to President George C. S. Benson of Claremont Men's College, whose interest and encouragement helped to make these seminars a reality, and to Mr. Fred Richman of Laguna Beach, California for his generous financial help in making the seminars possible.

As chairman of the 1966 seminars, Professor Martin Diamond was responsible for organizing the program.

Morton J. Frisch
Martin Diamond
1968

The
THIRTIES

Martin Diamond *is Burnet C. Wohlford Professor of American Political Institutions at Claremont Men's College and a former Fellow of the Center for Advanced Study in the Behavioral Sciences at Palo Alto, California. He is co-author of* The Democratic Republic *and* Essays in Federalism *and author of a number of essays on the* Federalist Papers.

Introduction

T HE AIM of the Seminars on the American Political Tradition is to supply a framework within which old problems become clearer and new problems become visible. In this year's seminars, inevitably and rightly our attention will be directed to the substance of specific problems—economics, militant movements, Franklin D. Roosevelt, labor, and literature. Here at the outset I will refer briefly to the underlying, and I hope, unifying theme of these seminars, namely, the American political tradition.

One aspect of that tradition was peculiarly tested and revealed in the Thirties. Consider the following: America is universally regarded as unique or pre-eminent in two things, the paradoxical relationship of which I call to your attention. We are, on the one hand, the country famed for swift, profound, and constant social change—the conquest of a continent, social mobility, the change from one vast farmland to a nation of the most modern cities, the insistent progress of technology. But while we are a country famed for our hospital-

[3]

ity to social change, we are, on the other hand, that modern nation which is pre-eminent for political stability. We have behind us two centuries of profound political stability and also two centuries of profound social change. How come? The explanation would teach us much about the meaning of the American political tradition. There is this clue: of all the decades in our experience, the Thirties is perhaps that decade above all in which social change and political stability had their harshest confrontation. The social and economic fears and wretchedness of that decade tested whether the American polity would continue to endure. During that decade and since, there especially emerged one of the enduring tensions of American political life—the conflict between those who were convinced, and even exulted in the conviction, that changing social necessity had rendered the old Constitution obsolete and those who were convinced, and shivered with delicious fright, that any new way of coping with social problems meant the instant demise of all that was constitutionally hallowed.

In contemplating the Thirties, we therefore consider an immensely important aspect of the American political experience, and indeed, of modernity in general—the relationship of social change and political stability or between the realm of society and the realm of the state—to use the modern terms for contemplating the human community. We consider accordingly whether the framers of the American Constitution succeeded in the intention attributed to them by Chief Justice Marshall in 1819 in a justly famous phrase. The framers, he said, devised a Constitution intended to endure for ages to come and consequently to be adapted to the various crises of human affairs. The Thirties presented America with one such profound crisis. We consider now whether those are right who believe modernity and its crises have radically outmoded the Constitution and its tradition, or those are right who preserve the past by preserving rigidly its practices and not flexibly its principles, or finally, whether those are right who see in the tradition something which outrode or mastered the crisis of the Thirties and which is a national source that, when combined with wisdom and moderation, may outride crises yet to come.

Martin Diamond

Claremont, California
February, 1966

Irving Kristol *is co-editor of the quarterly* The Public Interest *and Executive Vice-President of Basic Books, Inc. He was managing editor of* Commentary, *and co-founder and editor with Stephen Spender of* Encounter.

Ten Years in a Tunnel:
Reflection on the Thirties

I T SEEMS only yesterday; but even for those of us who have living and vivid memories of the Thirties, it remains a mystifying decade. This is not, I would suggest, a merely personal phenomenon. It involves the nation as a whole, for it derive· from—and touches upon—our confusion before some of the critical propositions of the American faith. How we interpret the Thirties will affect the way in which we interpret all preceding decades, and all subsequent ones, too. Coming to terms with the Thirties means coming to terms with the history and the prospects of American democracy itself. This is no easy matter, and it is not surprising that there is a general reluctance to think and write *seriously* about the Thirties.

Among younger people in the Sixties, an interest in the Thirties is, more often than not, an exercise in displaced nostalgia. It is very odd for those over 45, like myself, to hear their children strumming Woody Guthrie songs on a guitar, and singing mournfully of their grim experiences in the dust bowl or on the road. It is positively bizarre to hear them—middle-class youngsters all, who will probably never belong to a trade union in their lives—chanting what we used to call songs of social significance: all about wicked bosses and brutal strikebreakers and virtuous union maidens. The wicked bosses are probably their indulgent fathers; there aren't any strikebreakers any more; and if union maidens are virtuous these days, then the trade union movement is keeping this fact a secret.

Why do they do it? In part, I suppose, because this is the kind of pious homage that affluence always renders to simplicity. In part, too, I suppose, it is a case of mistaken identity—a confusion between the beatnik-bohemianism of the Sixties and the diverse miseries of the Thirties. The fact that the one is pleasantly liberating, whereas the other was most disagreeably constricting, is easily overlooked.

But above all, I should say that this strange nostalgia for what, everyone must agree, was a miserable period, derives from an intuitive recognition that the Thirties were America's last amateur decade. For if the United States in the Sixties is, as they say, a professional, organized society populated by organization men and women, then the United States in the Thirties was unquestionably, and in contrast, a nation of amateurs. Everything was amateurish about it: its economics, its politics, its foreign policy, even its radicalism. And precious little was organized in it, not even its miseries. This may commend the Thirties to young people today. But those of us who have had a first-hand acquaintance with these two decades will, I have no doubt, be unanimous in paraphrasing the current witticism: we've been disorganized and we've been organized, and believe me, being organized is better.

Outside of this peculiar nostalgia, which is largely confined to the young or the adolescent-minded, the general attitude toward the Thirties is one of smug superiority. There is no vision more acute than hindsight. As Edmund Burke observed long ago: "Men are wise with but little reflection, and good with little self-denial, in the business of all times except their own." And the general attitude of most people, looking back on the Thirties, can be summed up in the proposition: never were so many people so fantastically wrong about so many things. I happen to believe that this proposition is true enough. What I should like to warn against, however, is the notion that because we are in a position to appreciate the errors, and discern the follies, of the Thirties, we are thereby in a position to avoid similar errors and follies of our own. I do not believe for a moment that this is the case.

I think it is accurate to say that we have, in a way, "transcended" the particular idiocies of the Thirties. On the other hand, if we regard the Thirties as the decade in which American democracy suffered a nervous breakdown—and this, in effect, is what I think happened—it is not at all clear to me that the basic causes of this breakdown have been removed. As is the case with most successful recoveries from nervous breakdowns, the patient has now achieved an equilibrium of sorts—one that permits him to lead a useful and relatively calm existence—but only *relatively* calm and perhaps only *superficially* calm. The essential vulnerability is always there. And I think this vulnerability is all the greater, the more flippant, the more romantic, the more merely dismissive we are of that ghastly decade.

After all, the men of the Twenties—they, too, lived in a booming, prosperous, exuberant America, in which every dawn was rosier than the last—had no idea they were heading for ten years in a tunnel. When the darkness suddenly closed in, they couldn't understand it all. When the darkness suddenly closes in on us—as it surely will one day, for it always does (not the identical darkness, of course, but one just as shattering and oppressive)—when that occurs, will we understand it better? Which is to say, will we understand *ourselves* better? For profound social crises are not events that *happen* to us. They are not external "happenings"; we create them as we endure them.

The outer darkness is always but a reflection of an inner darkness—a black ignorance about our private and social selves—which we enlightened Americans are always shocked and astonished to discover is always *there*. What collapsed in 1929? What went wrong? Why were even the most severe critics of American society unprepared for the collapse, and why were they at a loss to explain it?

Let us take up this last question first, since it is the easiest to answer. Americans were at a loss to understand what was happening to them because, for the two decades prior to 1930, political philosophy and political theory—one might almost say political *thinking*—had practically ceased to exist in this country. In literature, in the arts, in cultural criticism in general, there was an upsurge of creativity and a quickening of interest. In politics there was nothing of the sort. After the Populist and Progressive movements had spent themselves, the American political mind sank into apathy. And from this apathy, it proceeded to move, in the Thirties, toward nightmare.

The political thought of the Populists and Progressives in the first decade of this century was neither majestic nor profound; but it *was* serious, and did grapple with some major issues—notably the growing inequality in the distribution of wealth and power in this country, as the result of the rapid growth of the corporation as an economic and social and political institution. Sometimes, as in the writings of Herbert Croly, it dared to challenge a fixed American idea—the Jeffersonian idea, for instance, that there was a primordial and enduring antagonism between society and the state, with society being a positive good and the state a necessary evil—society being the area of human freedom, the state being the area of human coercion—society emerging out of men's fraternal virtues, the state deriving from men's fratricidal vices.

I should like to quote a rather long paragraph from Croly's *The Promise of American Life,* published in 1912, because it so

perceptively defines a problem of the American political creed
that is basic to the American political experience of the past
fifty years. I quote:

> The substance of our national Promise has consisted . . . of an
> improving popular economic condition, guaranteed by democratic
> political institutions, and resulting in moral and social ameliora-
> tion. These manifold benefits were to be obtained merely by liberat-
> ing the enlightened self-interest of the American people. . . . The
> fulfillment of the American Promise was considered inevitable be-
> cause it was based upon a combination of self-interest and the
> natural goodness of human nature. On the other hand, if the
> fulfillment of our national Promise can no longer be considered
> inevitable, if it must be considered equivalent to a conscious na-
> tional purpose, instead of an inexorable national destiny, the impli-
> cation necessarily is that the trust reposed in individual self-interest
> has been in some measure betrayed. No preestablished harmony can
> then exist between the free and abundant satisfaction of private
> needs and the accomplishment of a morally and socially desirable
> result.

I think you can discern in this disjunction, outlined by Croly,
between the automatic national Promise and the conscious
national Purpose, between a society established exclusively on
the basis of individual self-interest and one established on
something that is larger, more comprehensive, more ambitious,
if you will, than individual self-interest—in this disjunction
there is to be found the central issue of American political life
in this century.

But by the Twenties, Croly was out of fashion, as was his
whole way of thinking. Not only was individual self-interest
unchallenged as the sublimest of American virtues; a wholly
frivolous and debased version of the doctrine of individual
self-interest was proclaimed as American orthodoxy, and was
almost universally accepted. The post-war years may have
thought they were returning to "business as usual," in the
old-fashioned American way. In fact, the Twenties saw the
American creed not reaffirmed, but transformed in a radical, if

subtle, way. If we wish to understand the silly radicalism of the Thirties, we must first comprehend the silly orthodoxy of the Twenties—by which I mean the ideological orthodoxy of Warren G. Harding, Calvin Coolidge, Herbert Hoover, and of the entire business community.

Now, the United States has always been a commercial society, and its values have always been those of a commercial civilization. But to say that is not to say so very much. A commercial civilization has many alternative ways of conceiving of itself, of defining itself—there is nothing automatic or unilinear about such self-definition. As the philosopher David Hume once observed; "Though men be much governed by interest, yet even interest itself, and all human affairs, are entirely governed by opinion." And the opinions which Americans have had about the essential qualities of their commercial civilization have changed very markedly in the past century and a half. On the whole, they have changed for the worse; and the Twenties witnessed what one might call the degradation of the commercial dogma.

For the better part of the 19th century, while success in business enterprise was highly valued and respected, this value and this respect fell short of simple idolatry. It was generally believed that success in business was related, in some important way, to the successful management of one's moral life. One became a success *because* one was frugal, sober, hard-working, devoted, self-denying, and pious; success was the *reward* for possessing these *virtues*. Those who made money without possessing these virtues were called "speculators," and—though one might have a grudging admiration for their talents—one did *not* have a candid respect for them as men or as citizens: *they* were definitely *not* the models of praiseworthy business enterprise, as is clear to anyone who will read the Horatio Alger novels.

But between the Civil War and the Great Depression, this connection between personal virtue and commercial success was steadily attenuated, and during the Twenties it became almost a parody of its former self. In this decade, the "speculator" inherited the earth—and the heavens above, too. It was no longer the virtuous man who made money; it was now money that made the virtuous man. This was no *sudden* transvaluation of values—the process was gradual, and covered many decades. But it culminated in the Twenties, by which time it was widely proclaimed and widely accepted as the new orthodoxy. No previous President could have dared to say, as Calvin Coolidge did say, that "the man who builds a factory builds a temple"—an earlier generation would have thought this remark at least mildly blasphemous. And in no other decade could Bruce Barton's book, *The Man Nobody Knows,* have become a raging best-seller—a book in which, as some of you might recall, Jesus and his apostles are solemnly celebrated as a brilliant organization of super-salesmen who, against overwhelming odds, managed to put over their commodity, Christianity, to the mass consumption audience of the Roman Empire.

Coincidental with this idolatry of the businessman, there was an upsurge of rabid anti-statism, of the most primitive and mindless kind. The serious writing and the serious thinking of the era of Theodore Roosevelt and of the early Woodrow Wilson were obliterated. There was not even a *reasoned* philosophy of the negative state. There was simply a blind, contemptuous, and utterly dogmatic distrust of government—especially of the federal government.

All of this left the American government, and the American business community, utterly defenseless before the crisis of the Great Depression. Whether the actions of this government and this community actually helped bring on the Depression is something historians may quarrel about. But what *is* indisputable is that this government and this community were childishly helpless in the face of it. And not merely helpless, but intellectually bankrupt as well: all that our leading businessmen and statesmen could say was that, in a depressed economy, it was more important than ever for the government to balance its budget. And they were not merely intellectually bankrupt, but morally corrupt as well, as subsequent investigation revealed. When William Gibbs McAdoo exclaimed in despair that "our entire banking system does credit to a collection of imbeciles," he was misstating the situation somewhat. It also did credit to a collection of cheats.

In 1929, the reigning ideology suffered a breakdown, and its representatives seem to have lost control, not only of the economic situation, but of themselves. Poor Herbert Hoover came to be the living symbol of this breakdown—and, one must say, he seemed to do everything in his power to earn this fate. In the early Twenties, he had been neither doctrinaire nor inflexible. He had then, for instance, advocated public works spending as an anti-cyclical measure in times of need; and Franklin D. Roosevelt had been so impressed by his enlightened views that he seriously regarded him as a potential *Democratic* candidate for President. Ten years later, however, Hoover was positively comic in his obstinate commitment to the shibboleths of the Twenties—assuring the nation that American hoboes were better fed than ever hoboes had been before; approving a $45,-000,000 appropriation to feed the livestock of Arkansas farmers, but disapproving, in the name of principle, a smaller appropriation to feed the farmers themselves and their families; telling the journalist, Raymond Clapper, that what the country needed most of all was "a good, big laugh."

Perhaps no single incident so neatly summed up the state of the nation on the eve of the New Deal as the testimony of Walter S. Gifford, President of A.T.&T. and head of the President's Organization on Unemployment Relief, before the U. S. Senate. Mr. Gifford informed the Senate that, although his committee had been in existence for several months, he had not the faintest notion how many people were unemployed, how many of these were getting relief, or how much relief they were getting. Moreover, his committee had made no effort to obtain any of this information! I doubt very much if one could find such a splendid exhibition of folly, on the part of a ruling class, on the eve of any major revolution in modern times. And it is a tribute to the sturdiness of American institutions, and to the infinite patience of the American citizenry, that we had no revolution of any kind, but merely the New Deal.

I say *merely* the New Deal because, while I should not want to depreciate the changes which the New Deal wrought in the American social, economic, and political order, I think it important to recognize that these changes, in the context of their times, were not particularly radical. The long-term influence of these changes has been most significant. But they had less direct impact on the Thirties than they have had indirect impact on us today. That so many Americans then regarded the New Deal as a dangerous, alien, and wickedly subversive regime is but another commentary on the decline in political thinking that had taken place in the previous five decades.

A similar commentary is provided by the reaction to the New Deal of a large portion of the intellectual community, who, under the influence of various Marxist fantasies, regarded the whole affair as the last capitalist frivolity before the inevitable apocalyptic deluge. I shall not linger over the dreary series of episodes which constitute the so-called "Red Decade" in American cultural life. After all, the Marxist intellectuals of the Thirties were no sillier, no more hysterical, than most of the reactionary businessmen of the period—and if anyone should say that intellectuals ought not, in the nature of the case, to be as silly as non-intellectuals, I can only reply that he has a most flattering, but utterly unrealistic conception of intellectuals as a class. As T. S. Eliot pointed out at the time, communism was, under the appalling circumstances, a perfectly *conventional* idea, "the natural idea for the thoughtless person." And intellectuals in politics can be both conventional and thoughtless—a fact disguised by their inclination to be *modishly* conventional and thoughtless.

In any case, the point I wish to emphasize is that the ideological opposition to the New Deal, whether of the Right or of the Left, was ephemeral in nature, if passionate in its conviction. I cannot offhand think of a single book, emerging out of the Right or Left of the Thirties that a historian of American political thought need refer to, except as a period piece.

As a matter of fact, one can say almost as much of the New Deal itself. Intellectually, the New Deal was not a particularly interesting enterprise. More than half the time, the New Deal seems not to have known what it was doing, or why it was doing it. Its great virtue, however, is that it did do *something*—it gave reassurance to the American people that their government was not indifferent to their needs or incapable of coping with their problems. And such reassurance was, at the time, most desperately needed.

After all, to the American people trapped in the Great Depression, there was one obvious fact about their situation—namely, it was completely and irredeemably absurd. *Here* were men without work—men willing to work on any terms. Here were families without food. *There* were idle factories, untilled farmlands. The innocent and inescapable question was: why not join the "here" and the "there" into productive enterprise? Both the Left and the Right had ingeniously complicated explanations as to why this was not possible. But, as we now know, it was perfectly possible all along. It has been said that there would have been no Great Depression, and certainly not one lasting a decade, if the economists had, earlier on, paid due attention to the writings of John Maynard Keynes. This is doubtless correct. But I think it would also be correct to say that the Depression would not have been so severe as it was, or lasted as long as it did, if there had been no economists around at all. The problem was so clear-cut, the solution so apparent, that one had to be a scholar *not* to see it.

Franklin D. Roosevelt, thank God, was no scholar, and he never could understand economics. True, he had scholars and experts all around him. But he did not listen too attentively to most of them; and there are grounds for thinking that, if he had listened less, the Depression would have been over somewhat sooner.

There were, essentially, three liberal schools of thought that fused into the New Deal and its various programs. The first was the Keynesian school, with its great emphasis on fiscal policy. The members of this school were not, on the whole, very prominent, and the doctrines of that school seemed too good to be true, too easy to be true; unhappily, the New Deal acted upon them only in a half-hearted and intermittent way. The second school, which we may call the Brandeis-Frankfurter school, continued the tradition of Wilson's "New Freedom," with its emphasis on trust-busting, the harassment of big business, and the restoration of individual enterprise as the condition of liberty and equality. A third school, continuing the tradition of Teddy Roosevelt's "Bull Moose" crusade, and represented by Rexford Tugwell, A. A. Berle, and others, emphasized government regulation and even some kind of governmental planning. The reforms these last two groups brought about were, on the whole, desirable. But most economists today, I think, would agree that they had precious little effect on the Depression, and that the enjoyment of their benefits was largely the privilege of the post-World War II era. Economists are always combatting yesterday's crisis, just as generals are always fighting yesterday's war. And most of the liberal economists of the Thirties were concerned with translating into reality the progressive programs of 1912. These programs concerned mainly the *distribution* of wealth and power in the American commonwealth, not the *creation* of wealth and power. Their passion was for social justice; and they tended to regard economic revival as a function of social justice, which, alas, it is not—at least not necessarily. As events turned out, economic revival was a function of war.

There was, however, one New Deal thinker who did, in fact, represent something new. He was not terribly influential. But he was highly popular among younger academics, and his cast of mind foreshadowed some of the more salient and disagreeable characteristics of the post-war era. I refer to Thurman Arnold, whose *Folklore of Capitalism* is, I believe, still in print, though it seems not to receive much attention. In its day, it had quite an impact. It attacked all of the prevalent ideologies, including—perhaps even especially—the liberal ones. It was sarcastic, sardonic, antimoralistic, exceedingly tough-minded, and highly skeptical of American pieties and democratic slogans. Its point of view was managerial; it saw and it celebrated the statesman as a "policy scientist," manipulating the mass of self-seeking and hypocritical people for their own good. Had Franklin D. Roosevelt taken the book seriously, the Thirties in the United States might really have witnessed a transformation of American politics and of the American way of life—though not a particularly desirable one, except perhaps in the eyes of a few would-be Machiavelli's. But Franklin Roosevelt, despite his friendship for Thurman Arnold and his willingness to give him a fairly high government position, never took his ideas seriously.

As a matter of fact, F. D. R. never took too seriously *any* of the unemployed ideas that were then drifting idly through the country; and that was his great accomplishment. When most of the prevailing ideas are bad, there can be political virtue in pragmatism. Franklin D. Roosevelt very nicely fits Walter Bagehot's description of the constitutional statesman: "a nature at once active and facile, easily acquiring opinions from without, not easily devising them from within, a large placid adaptive intellect. . . ." When the nominating conventions met in 1932, at a moment of great national emergency, the most controversial and time-consuming issue at *both* the Democratic and Republican conventions was the repeal of prohibition. This was obviously not a nation that was intellectually or spiritually ready for any large rethinking of its political life and its political institutions. It *was* ready for bold action, but only within a limited framework. It wanted limited experimentation, carried out with the greatest possible vigor and gusto, and this Franklin Roosevelt gave them. His genius—and I use that term advisedly—was his ability to inspire in the American people the confidence that all his programs, no matter how bewildering and novel they appeared at the moment, were simply extensions of the philosophy of the founding fathers. He rooted American liberalism in a deeper American conservatism, and thereby prepared the way for the liberal regimes of the subsequent twenty years.

Oddly enough, the one problem he coped with least effectually is the one that, in the eyes of succeeding generations, he is regarded as having coped with best—namely, the Depression. He was far too much a prisoner of the prevailing economic fallacies to cope with that. The proposition that the best government budget is a balanced budget was one he could never challenge, even while he violated its injunction. It really made no sense to him, any more than it did to most Americans of the decade, that when times are bad the government should be more spendthrift than when times are good. That seemed too perverse a paradox. As a result, in 1940, the United States was still very much in the Depression. In that year, John Maynard Keynes wrote an article in *The New Republic* which surveyed the American experience of the past ten years and came to a mournful conclusion: "It seems politically impossible," he wrote, "for a capitalist democracy to organize expenditure on the scale necessary to make the grand experiment which would prove my case—except in war conditions." He went on to say that perhaps the establishment of a war economy, then in its initial stages, would be, and I quote, "the stimulus, which neither the victory nor the defeat of the New Deal could give you, to greater consumption and a higher standard of life." The war, as we know, did precisely that. It was thereafter impossible, and will forever more be impossible, to pretend that what the government could achieve in wartime—namely, a full employment of economic resources—was beyond its wit and its power in peacetime.

I do not want to seem to be running down the significance of the New Deal. I wish only to try to understand that significance properly. The New Deal certainly laid the foundations of what we now call the welfare state, with its laws on social security, the minimum wage, unemployment insurance, and so on. It certainly laid the foundations of what we now call the affluent society, with its reliance upon energetic government to encourage economic growth. It did all of these things *for us;* but it did not solve its own problem of the Depression. One might reasonably speculate that it would eventually have done so, even had the war not come along. But this remains speculation, not history.

This point is worth emphasizing because one of the effects of the New Deal, and of the boom years that followed it, has been to fix in the public mind a mythical connection between welfare legislation and economic prosperity—between the welfare state and the affluent society. Now I do not wish to be misunderstood: not only do I have no objections to welfare legislation, I *approve* of the idea of the welfare state in principle. But the fact remains that social welfare legislation is one thing, and economic prosperity is another. A great many people are convinced that without minimum wage laws, or strong trade unions, or social security, you cannot have an economy working at the level of full employment. I do not know of any professional economist who would entertain this thesis. You could abolish all the social welfare legislation of the New Deal tomorrow, and—*if* the government took appropriate compensatory fiscal action—it need not adversely affect the workings of the economy as a whole. In the Thirties we had much social legislation and little prosperity. We now could, in the abstract, have little or no welfare legislation and much prosperity. Nothing of the sort is going to happen, of course, but the distinction is worth keeping in mind because it permits us to achieve a clearer perception of the political principles of the welfare state; to distinguish them from the economic principles of the affluent society, and to appreciate the peculiar way in which these two sets of principles have been wedded to one another as a result of the New Deal.

Back in 1932, during his electoral campaign, Franklin D. Roosevelt said in a speech: "As I see it, the task of government in its relation to business is to assist the development of an economic declaration of rights, an economic constitutional order. . . ." This identification of a constitutional order with a declaration of rights has deep roots in the American past: one might even say it is the basic metaphysical proposition of American liberalism. Perhaps F. D. R. meant nothing very substantial by this statement; it is the sort of thing a liberal politician is expected to say at election time. But as the New Deal developed, a new conception of economic rights *did* make its appearance—the conception of group rights as against merely individual rights. Whereas the older American credo was individualistic, the new one was oriented toward *organized interests.* "Equal opportunity for all" and "fair shares for all" used to refer, before the New Deal, to individual opportunities and individual shares. During the Thirties this individualism was superseded by a perspective which saw American society in terms of organized groups—trade unions, farmers, old people, Negroes, schoolteachers, students, small businessmen, large businessmen, sick people, veterans, and the like. And American economic life—and much of our political life, too—came to be and still is, the negotiating of acceptable arrangements among all these groups.

In the early days of the New Deal there was the traditional progressive chatter about "the vested interests," and how they were arrogantly frustrating the will, and mischievously blasting the happiness of the common man. Since what Croly called "the American Promise" took for granted that there was a natural and pre-established harmony between the individual's self-interest and society's well-being, some explanation was needed to help explain away the obvious and embarrassing fact that this harmony as often as not just did not exist. The idea of a "vested interest" supplied the necessary explanation—a vested interest being an organized group that used its power in such a way as to gain special privileges for its members, at the expense of ordinary, innocent, and unorganized individuals. What the New Deal did, however, was to begin the process of converting the American people from a mere collection of random individuals into a nation-wide pattern of vested interests. The New Deal did indeed sketch out a new economic declaration of rights. It never candidly proclaimed it, of course—no American government has done that since, for that matter, the old individualist mythology is still too powerful—but it did help establish it. And the nature of this innovation can be summed up saying that whereas American government used to be committed to securing "equal rights for all," it was now committed—it *is* now committed—to securing "equal privileges for all." We are all vested interests now!

So strong is our individualistic bias, that it is difficult even to describe this process without sounding censorious and disapproving. In fact, quite a few people who had an early and enthusiastic association with the New Deal found such a revision of the charter of American economic rights and liberties profoundly objectionable. Many of the older progressives did not at all like the "collectivist" bias that became ever more evident in the New Deal's programs. Their dislike was soon transformed into disillusionment, and eventually into bitter opposition. For myself, I should like to make it clear that I think this change was inevitable; and while moralists and poets have every right to protest against the inevitable, I do not think it proper for a mere political analyst to do so. Modern industrial society and modern government is inherently moved toward large-scale organization. One might reasonably debate the limits that ought to be imposed on this movement in any particular case, at any particular moment. But to argue against the tendency itself, or to wish to reverse it, is to indulge in the politics of romanticism. And as you may have gathered, I am not the romantic type.

But this new society of vested interests is still not a constitutional *order,* because the rights of these various groups have not been attached to any corresponding set of obligations. In truth, our new society is even less of a constitutional order than the old one. For, while there was once thought to be a mystical harmony between individual self-interest and the common good, individual self-interest itself was frankly recognized to be limited by a *moral* discipline. As I have pointed out, the moral dimension of American individualism has slowly been withering away, until by the Twenties it had become a mocking shadow of its former self. Nevertheless, it never entirely disappeared—if only because simple patriotism did not allow it to. Thus, the apostles of American individualistic self-interest have always agreed, at the very least, that the individual ought to be ready to lay down his life for his country. To reconcile this belief with the idea that the individual is, and ought to be motivated only by self-interest, requires some intellectual acrobatics. But, whether or not this reconciliation made any logical sense, it was nevertheless accomplished. By some sophistry or other, or simply by disregarding their own inconsistency, all those who proclaimed that individual self-interest is the sacred and inviolable principle of human behavior, that it was the supreme American *right* to be self-interested, still believed it proper for our schools and our churches to teach their members that this same self-interested individual should, under suitable circumstances, commit an act of disinterested civic virtue.

When you substitute organized groups for individuals, however, it is far more difficult to incorporate *any* moral qualities into political life. The self-interest of a group is a much more powerful principle than the self-interest of an individual. It is less ready to brook inconsistencies, it is more immune to rhetorical persuasion. The sentiments of a group are always more crass and vulgar and materialistic than the sentiments of an individual. After all, one knows sentimental businessmen, sentimental trade union leaders, sentimental professors even. But there is no such thing as a sentimental corporation, a sentimental trade union, or a sentimental university. These collectivities are, in the nature of the case, what we call "hard-headed."

How, out of the competition and conflict of these hard-headed collectivities, can one sustain a decent social and political order? If one turns to our economists and political scientists for an answer, one sometimes gets the impression that they have given up hope of ever answering this question in a rational way. They cannot, without seeming silly, propose any kind of mystical harmony between the interests of all groups and a common good, a public interest. So what they fall back on, most of the time, is the equilibrium of the jungle, in which each predatory creature, following its own unfettered instincts, achieves some kind of ecological balance with all the other predatory creatures. The principle of countervailing power becomes the operating principle of modern industrial society. What they forget, of course, is that man is a *political* animal, one who has created civilized society precisely because the law of the jungle is repugnant to his deepest instincts rather than expressive of them. Even if it were theoretically possible to have a social order governed entirely by countervailing power, unmitigated by any nobler or higher aspect, the question still remains: why should a human being wish to live in such a social order?

This question our welfare state does not pretend to answer. It accepts implicitly the notions that group interests are the fundament of our social order, and that there is no "public interest" except as it emerges from the competitive activities—economic and political—of these group interests. But the welfare state does have a way of keeping this competitive struggle within bounds. It achieves this through the affluent society. That is to say, the welfare state undertakes responsibility for sustained and continuous economic growth. The more wealth society creates, the more there is to go around, the less likelihood there is of any one group being disadvantaged to an extreme. There is even the possibility of using some of this wealth to help those interest groups who do not make out so well on their own efforts. A rich society can afford to be benevolent, even if benevolence is not one of its essential principles.

This combination of welfare state and affluent society—this high regard for the interest of all groups and this determined commitment to economic growth and expansion—this is what American society and the American polity have become since the Depression and the New Deal. This is our "new order." There is, clearly, a great deal to be said in its favor: contrasted with the Twenties and the Thirties, the Forties, Fifties, and Sixties must be accorded a suitable measure of respect, if not reverence. If they have not been among the noblest of decades, they have not been among the worst, either.

We are nevertheless entitled to ask—we are nevertheless obliged to ask—how secure is this achievement? How stable is this new combination of welfare state and affluent society? What are its prospects? And when we try to speculate about possible answers to these questions, we are struck by two things.

First, a commitment to economic growth is a promissory note that we shall find increasingly burdensome in the years to come. Trees stop growing short of the heavens, and economic growth never reaches infinity. If the United States were to have a continuous rate of economic growth of 3.5% a year—a rate now generally regarded as rather modest—our standard of living would double in twenty years, would be multiplied 31 times in the next 100 years, and be multiplied 961 times at the end of two centuries! It may be that I am insufficiently imaginative, but I just do not think this marvellous multiplication is going to happen. *Something* will go wrong; and when that happens, how will we react? How severe will be our "withdrawal symptoms," once economic growth ceases to give us ever new "highs"? These are disturbing questions that it is not, perhaps, premature to entertain.

Secondly, the welfare state and affluent society do not resolve the problem of the *quality* of American life. Even if the reliance on group self-interest can achieve, more securely than a reliance on individual self-interest, a prosperous and relatively stable society, can it achieve anything we should like to call a "good society"? Not a *great* society, but a *good* society—a society whose best representatives, at least, are representative of the best that the human race can achieve. Just how satisfying are the principles of our society to a thinking man, or a man of spirit? Are our young people and future generations going to remain content with a materialistic ethos? Will they blandly accept the proposition that social justice means nothing more than fair shares for all—or even equal privileges for all? Noticing some of the recent happenings on our university campuses, I infer that this question is not entirely academic.

So what it comes down to—what it always comes down to—is at what point will the Promise of American life be compelled to yield before the Purpose of American life? We have, today, a somewhat different promise from that of the pre-New Deal era.

But will that promise be any more self-sustaining? Or will it, too, lead to disillusionment, distress, and a demand for radical revision?

Lord Percy of Newcastle once said: "A sovereign people who cannot find a way to express their virtues in a strong national government may . . . sublimate their vices in a weak one." To which we can add the amendment: it may even sublimate their vices in a *strong* one. We can all agree, I'm sure, that sublimated vices are the best kinds of vices. But I should like to think we would also agree that, in politics as in life, the sublimation of vices is not quite the same thing as virtue, and is, indeed, inferior to it.

Howard Zinn *is Professor of Government at Boston University. He has published* La Guardia in Congress, *a Beveridge Prize publication of the American Historical Association,* The Southern Mystique, SNCC, The New Abolitionists *and has edited* New Deal Thought.

A Comparison of the Militant Left of the Thirties and Sixties

To SPEAK of the militant left of the Thirties is to recall the magnificent procession that opens a bull fight. The bull in this metaphor represents the business ethic of Harding, Coolidge, Hoover. Into the ring parade the various fighters: the *picadors* who ride tired horses and infuriate the bull with lances (who are these, the Communists?) ; the *banderilleros,* who use brilliant-colored barbed darts to enrage the bull (are these the Trotskyists?) ; the *toreros,* who distract the bull by waving red flags (the Norman Thomas Socialists?). And who is the matador—dashing, glamorous, smiling, deadly, a lion and a fox— Franklin D. Roosevelt? It is the matador who kills the bull. The crowd applauds, forgetting momentarily that there is an endless succession of bulls, and tomorrow another matador will

[27]

appear, asking applause (who is this, John F. Kennedy, Lyndon Johnson?). And who are the new *picadors, banderilleros, toreros?* SNCC? SDS? The May 2nd Movement? The DuBois Clubs? Martin Luther King? Mario Savio? Staughton Lynd? And do we dare ask, when everyone has left the arena and the crowds have gone home, what remains in the ring besides a certain quantity of dead bull?

This is all too flippant, of course. The antics of the old Left are an easy target for ridicule—the stage whispering and the posturing, the dogma; the in-fighting; the Talmudic debates among Trotskyists, Communists, Lovestonites, old Wobblies; the hypocrisy; the self-righteousness. But measure these defects against the evils which the Left saw in the Thirties: the hungry children, the evicted families shivering in the streets, the men standing in long lines for a day's work, the Negroes lynched in the South and jammed into filthy ghettos in the North. All this happened in the richest nation, the most liberal nation in the world. And overseas, the Japanese were butchering China, Mussolini's tanks rumbling towards Ethiopian farmers carrying spears, German warplanes bombing Barcelona, Hitler beginning the deadly round-up of the Jews and raving in the Sportspalast in Berlin. And all this happened while Western Christian countries hemmed and hawed and murmured about Communism.

In the Roosevelt circle itself there was no one we could call a militant Leftist, despite the cries of the Chamber of Commerce, Father Coughlin and the Liberty League, despite Al Smith saying that behind the New Dealers were really Norman Thomas, Karl Marx and Lenin, and asking: "Who is Ickes? Who is Wallace? Who is Hopkins, and in the name of all that is good and holy, who is Tugwell, and where did he blow from?" Tugwell, of all in the inner Roosevelt group, was the boldest in his economic analysis, calling (as early as 1932 in a paper to the American Economic Association) for national economic planning and the control of prices and profits, which meant, he said, that "business will logically be required to disappear."

We would need to move outside the Roosevelt official family to find Leftist intellectuals in any number more than one. There is John Dewey, whose pragmatism went beyond that of FDR to embrace an attack on the profit system. There's Upton Sinclair, with his mild, homey American brand of socialism, saying that "in a cooperative society every man, woman, and child would have the equivalent of $5000 a year income from the labor of men who worked for three or four hours a day." Reinhold Niebuhr urged that "private ownership of the productive processes" be abandoned. Harvard philosopher William Ernest Hocking asked for "collectivism of a sort," but neither the collectivism of a "headless liberalism" or of a "heady" communism or fascism. Paul Douglas, then an economist at the University of Chicago, called for organization of the weak and poor to force FDR's hand and move him towards a bolder program.

When we speak of the *militant* Left, however, we must move from the professors to the students, from the intellectuals to the labor organizers, from the lecture platform to the picket line. We must take in the demonstrations of the unemployed, the farmers violently preventing foreclosures, the workers boarding streetcars and refusing to pay fare, or those 55 people in Chicago who were charged with dismantling an entire four-story building and carrying it away, brick by brick. We find those who moved the furniture of evicted families back into the tenements in New York City, and those who sailed off to fight in the Spanish Civil War.

In that crazy, billowing, tangled web of the Left, I want to single out for comparison with today's radicals one key strand, or perhaps one set of strands—the Communist-influenced Left. The Left of the Thirties was much more than this, but I have two reasons for concentrating on this segment of the Left. First, it was undoubtedly stronger, more influential than the rest. Second, the comparison with today's radicals is more than academic exercise; it may throw light on the accusations sometimes made against the New Left: that they are either secretly Communists, or infiltrated by Communists, or sympathetic to Maoism.

The Communist Party reported 12,000 members in 1932, and about 80,000 at the end of the decade. The turnover was quick, and in the Thirties perhaps 100,000 or even 200,000 Americans moved in and out of the Party, so that we might say several hundred thousand were directly influenced by Communist ideas. These people worked in the more militant unions of the C.I.O., in the American Student Union and the American Youth Congress, in fraternal orders like the International Workers Order, in civil rights groups like the National Negro Congress, in foreign policy groups like the American League Against War and Fascism.

It is with the Communist-influenced militant Left of the Thirties that I would like to compare the New Left of the Sixties. To represent this New Left, while recognizing that there are other groups which might be considered part of it, I would discuss those elements I know best: the Student Nonviolent Coordinating Committee, which is the most aggressive of the civil rights groups working in the South; Students for a Democratic Society, which carries on a variety of activities on campuses, in depressed urban areas, on civil rights and foreign policy; and that assorted group of intellectuals, civil rights workers and just ordinary draft-card burners who have become active in the opposition to the war in Vietnam.

Before noting the differences between the Old Left and the New Left, we should recognize the common ground which they share. Both have been sharply, angrily critical of American society, at home and abroad. Both movements of the Thirties and of the Sixties have pointed to poverty in the midst of wealth, to sins committed against the Negro, to limitations on

free expression by Congressional committees and public prose-
cutors, to shameful behavior in foreign policy. And in this, both
movements I believe—despite many characteristics which I find
distasteful in the Old Left and mostly missing in the New
Left—have made vital contributions to values in American
society which almost all of us claim to cherish.

I see, first, in the new militants, a lack of ideology unthink-
able in the Old Left. Alfred Kazin has spoken (in his book
Starting Out in The Thirties) of many Leftists in his time as
"ideologues." They were always attending classes on Marxist
theory, buying or selling or arguing about works by the Big
Four (Marx, Engels, Lenin, Stalin) , engaging in endless discussions on surplus value, dialectical materialism, the absolute
impoverishment of the working class. Plekhanov's theory on
the role of the individual, Stalin's views on the national question, Engels on the origin of the family, Lenin on economism,
or imperialism, or social democracy, or the state as the executive committee of the bourgeoisie.

The people in SNCC, by and large, know little about Marx.
They have no Manifesto or any other infallible guide to the
truth. Their discussions are rarely abstract or theoretical, and
deal mostly with day-to-day practical problems: the tent city in
Lowndes County, hunger in Greenville, the Freedom Democratic Party, how to meet the next payroll for the 130 field
secretaries. SDS people I have met are more white than SNCC,
more middle-class, more intellectual, and thus have read more
of Marx—but they don't seem to take it as the Gospel. I recently read a book of essays by SDS people, and found very
little theorizing in it, above the level of the immediate. The
Old Left would have had a quotation from Lenin on the head-
quarters wall. In the dilapidated SNCC offices, you will find
odd bits of prose and poetry pinned on the walls, like this,
which I saw recently in Atlanta:

> *Ever danced out on a limb*
> *It doesn't always break.*

And sometimes when it does you fall
into a grassy meadow.

All this means there is an open-mindedness and a flexibility in
the New Left which was rare in the Thirties. There is a refresh-
ing lack of pompous intellectuality, of quotations from the
great, of hewing to a "line." To some people on borders of the
Left today, like Michael Harrington, the lack of ideology is
disturbing. I admit I have some tremors from time to time, but
on the whole I find it heartening.

The Old Left was rigidly committed to a nation and to a
system: the nation was the Soviet Union, and the system was
socialism. Some adherents were disillusioned by Stalin's purges
of old Bolsheviks in the Thirties; others dropped away after the
non-aggression pact between the USSR and Germany. But
many stood fast, held by the power of an earlier vow which they
were unwilling to renounce. This new generation of radicals
starts with no such commitment. They have no illusions about
the purity of any nation, any system. They have seen Stalinism
unmasked, by Khrushchev himself. They have watched aggression, subversion, and double-dealing engaged in by all sides,
West as well as East, "free world" as well as "communist
world." They are very much aware of Russian aggression in
Hungary, Chinese repression in Tibet, and the desire of Communists everywhere to support revolution in the world. But
they also know that the American CIA overthrew a democrati-
cally-elected government in Guatemala, that the United States
secretly conspired in the invasion of Cuba, that our marines
invaded the Dominican Republic in violation of the Rio Pact.
The new radicals are quite persuaded that the Communist
nations will use *any* means to gain their ends. Yet, when they
see American planes bombing Vietnamese villages, and marines throwing grenades down tunnels in which crouch helpless
women and children, they see that the United States will use
any means to gain *its* ends. They have grown up in a world
where force and deception are found on all sides; and so they

have what I believe is a healthy disposition to call the shots as they see them, no matter who looks bad.

The Old Left was sectarian, suspicious, and exclusive: the Socialists would expel Communists, the Trotskyists would expel Socialists, and the Communists would expel almost everyone. While there is some silly back-biting in SNCC against other civil rights groups, both SNCC and SDS are open organizations, welcoming anyone regardless of affiliation or ideology who will work. One result is a succession of head-shakings and warnings from various people about Communist infiltrators (this is the liberal counterpart of Communist suspiciousness), but SNCC and SDS have remained cool on this subject. Bob Moses of SNCC, in the fall of 1963, responded to an article by Theodore White in *Life Magazine,* where White referred accusingly to a "penetration" of SNCC by "unidentified elements." White seemed bashful about saying he meant Communists. Moses replied: "It seems to me that . . . we have to throw what little weight we have on the side of free association and on the side of autonomy within our group to pick and choose those people whom we will work with, on relevant criteria, and one of the criteria which is not relevant is their past political associations." Another SNCC veteran, Charles Sherrod, said: "I don't care who the heck it is—if he's willing to come down on the front lines and bring his body along with me to die—then he's welcome!"

The radicals of the Thirties were dutiful bureaucrats: over-organized, over-prompt, and quite parliamentary. If a SNCC worker cited Roberts Rules of Order, non-violence would probably be ditched for that moment. The B'nai Brith or the Elks have been known to start their meetings fifteen minutes late, and the Young Democrats of Waukegan an hour late, but SNCC often starts meetings a day late, sometimes two. I am not citing this as a virtue, but rather as a sign of that human carelessness about organization which seemed to be lacking in the Old Left. A bureaucratic sense of "responsibility" is largely

a product of middle-class upbringing, and SNCC is more prole-
tarian-peasant in background than either SDS, the teach-in
crowd, or the Old Left.

The radicals of the Thirties indulged in a good deal of
hero-worship, from Stalin over there to Earl Browder over here.
Today's militants, on the other hand, are suspicious of individuals who set themselves up, or are set up by others, as heroes of
the movement. That is one reason SNCC is critical of Martin
Luther King, Jr. Neither SNCC nor SDS nor the New Left as a
whole has some one person immediately identifiable as *the*
leader. It is hard to fit Bob Moses or John Lewis or Tom
Hayden or Carl Oglesby into the pattern of a charismatic
figure, and while the mass media have tried to do this with
Staughton Lynd, both he and others in the New Left have
derided this.

There is an existential quality to current radicalism which
distinguishes it sharply from that of the Thirties. Marxists,
particularly the dogmatic ones, are rather unhappy with existentialism, even though Jean-Paul Sartre has made an attempt
to reconcile his existentialism with his Marxism. (Walter
Odajnyk's study of this attempt finds it unsuccessful.) To discover what separates the orthodox Left of the Thirties from
existentialism, see a new book by a Marxist, Sidney Finkelstein,
called *Existentialism and Alienation in American Literature.*
Finkelstein finds the Existentialist insufficiently aware of the
binding force of history, incredulous of the idea of progress,
excessively emotional, overly individualist, and, as he puts it,
"the modern counterpart of the ancient rebel against a world
he saw as corrupt, who withdrew to a cave or monastery."

Let's first take the charge of emotionalism. Blaise Pascal had
said is his *Pensées,* in the middle of the 17th century: "The
heart has its reasons, which reason does not know. . . ." This
seems like such sentimental spirituality, so ineffective (and we
demand *effectiveness* today) in a cold world of Realpolitik, so
subversive of that iron-clad reason which marks modern man

and particularly the modern atheistic radical. Now we must recognize that the point of ignition of the new radicalism was the civil rights movement, and this movement has been an emotional one, as anyone who has ever attended a mass meeting in a Negro church in the deep South knows. But it seems to me one of the contributions of the new radicalism is to show that such emotionalism is not destructive of rationality, that passion in itself is morally neutral, capable of supporting any value, and that when it is attached to a humane cause it *contributes* to rational action. It does this because verbal discourse alone is a pale reflection of life, inadequate to convey the anguish that human beings feel; words need to be intensified by emotion to more accurately describe the reality of both suffering and joy.

Emotion plays not only this kind of supporting role for rational decision-making; it also has an initiating role in moral decisions. The logical positivists, from Hume to Hans Reichenbach, have told us we cannot rationally deduce first statements about what *should* be. But we may very well *feel* them. And there is a shared feeling among people about certain basic values, which should not be discarded because it cannot, in the academic sense, be "proved." We *know,* we *feel,* that peace is preferable to war, nourishment to starvation, brotherhood to enmity, that it is better to be free than to be in jail, better to love than to hate, better to live than to die. And yet—this is the devilish power of human communication, the curse of language—we can be taught, *rationally,* that war is preferable to peace (all we ask is a few words of explanation from those on high who know and can soothe our troubled minds) ; that jail is preferable to freedom (due process and judicial respectability calm our indignation) ; that starvation is better than nourishment (for others, of course, so we accept the destruction of crops if it is "the enemy's" crop) . When we see the bombing of a fishing village, because it is suspected of being a Communist resting area, we *feel* this is wrong, but we are soon persuaded

rationally that this must be. There are Soviet citizens, I am
sure, who *feel* that it is wrong to send two writers to jail for
what they have written; but the calm, reasonable explanations
go forth and the feeling is smothered, or at least suppressed. Is
it any wonder that this new generation of radicals has such a
distrust of this perversion of "reason," that they are willing to
trust their emotions in deciding what is right and what is
wrong? Let me quote one of the original SNCC organizers, a
young white girl from Virginia named Jane Stembridge:

> . . . finally it all boils down to human relationships. It has nothing
> to do finally with governments. It is the question of whether we . . .
> whether *I* shall go on living in isolation or whether there shall be a
> we. The student movement is not a cause . . . it is a collision
> between this one person and that one person. It is a *I am going to
> sit beside you.* . . . Love alone is radical. Political statements are
> not; programs are not; even going to jail is not. . . .

The radicals of the Thirties believed fervently in the power
of historical forces churning away, moving the world inexora-
bly towards a glorious future. This came from the historical
materialism of Marxism, with its confident laying-out of the
stages of history. Capitalism would be followed by socialism
just as surely as it had followed feudalism. Socialism would be
the first stage of communism which would be a return in one
sense to an earlier primitive communalism, but in a more
important sense would represent a complete break with the
impoverished past. All would be pre-history; man's life as a free
human being would truly begin now, with communism, and he
would for the first time take charge of his own destiny, become
the prime motive power in the movement of history. It was a
ferocious determinism, and yet, oddly enough, it was accompanied by the most vigorous calls to action. This should have
made its adherents suspicious of the notion of "inevitability"
which pervades Marxism, but they accepted this dialectical
"unity of opposites" as dutifully as Calvinists accompanied the

notion of predestination with exhortations to moral behavior.

The radicals I know today are not bound by history. They accept neither the Marxist nor the Biblical nor any other interpretation of history. What they know best is the present, and they consider it malleable by the power of their own hands. When you have *made* history, when you have *forced* social change, the magic of a philosophy of history fades. In eleven years, if we date the movement from the Montgomery Bus Boycott of 1955, or six years, if we date it from the sit-ins of February, 1960, the militant youngsters of the Southern movement have moved mountains—not very far, true, but to move a mountain even a few inches gives a sense of power. "The Deep South Says Never," a journalist wrote after the Supreme Court decision. But Negroes are defying guns and subterfuge in Alabama and Mississippi, organizing their own parties, preparing to elect their own sheriffs, mayors, congressmen. In Georgia, Negroes are sitting in the state legislature, and the expulsion of Julian Bond can be seen not only as a patriotic move to support the Vietnamese war by the freedom-loving members of the Georgia General Assembly, but also as a belated outburst of anger at the thought of so many Negroes sitting among them in their formerly sacrosanct, all-white chamber. Southern Negroes are still poor, but they dare to strike in the Mississippi Delta against the plantation owner. They are still afraid, but not as afraid as they used to be. The active ones know that the changed atmosphere is not the result of beneficence from the succession of Great White Fathers in Washington, but the result of their own willingness to risk their lives, to march, to demonstrate, to go to jail; they know that Johnson and Kennedy did not act for them, but reacted to them. These Southern militants feel free to change history. And although they know they have only scratched the surface of a social order which keeps them poor and harassed, they are off their knees; they have stretched their limbs, and are ready to do more, undeterred by notions of what history does or does not permit them to do.

Yet, when the hold of history is weakened, it allows not only awareness of freedom, but a sense of despair. This is very much in the existentialist mood, and quite different from the radicalism of the Thirties. To the old radicals, revolution was always around the corner; the proletariat was always about to rise and smite the foe; capitalism was always about to collapse in one of its periodic economic crises; every bloody nose received by the Left was received not with a call for a handkerchief, but with joy that here was a sign of the desperation of the reactionaries, and so the day of socialism was not far off.

The New Left is not afraid to say it is unsure of victory. In Tom Hayden's piece in *The New Republic* he makes no cheery predictions about how SDS will transform America, and says: "Radicalism then would go beyond the concepts of optimism and pessimism as guides to work, finding itself in working despite odds. Its realism and sanity would be grounded in nothing more than the ability to face whatever comes." Michael Harrington, commenting on this, is unhappy; he needs to know he will win, and right away, and so seeks desperately to create a coalition which will have a majority of Americans in it. Harrington still has much of the Old Left in him. The new radical is more in tune with Wendell Phillips, the abolitionist orator, who wrote: "The reformer is careless of numbers, disregards popularity, and deals only with ideas, conscience, and common sense. . . . He neither expects, nor is overanxious for immediate success." Phillips contrasted the reformer with the politician, who "dwells in everlasting now. . . ." Similarly, James Russell Lowell, the abolitionist poet, wrote: "The Reformer must expect comparative isolation, and he must be strong enough to bear it." The new radicals' strength comes from the other side of existentialist despair, a supreme sense of responsibility, an unrelenting activism.

The radicals of the Thirties were very active in traditional politics. They ran candidates and sought entry into legislative bodies. William Z. Foster and Earl Browder were the Communist candidates for President at various times; Norman Thomas was the perennial Socialist candidate. Their realism about parliamentary democracy did not seem to be even as penetrating as that of conservative political scientists, who quietly point out the flaws in the electoral process. It is a fact of American political life that the cards are stacked against minority candidates in our electoral college system, and in the single-district system by which we elect Congressmen. And even if a radical should break through, mysterious things begin to happen. Socialist Victor Berger, twice elected, was twice excluded from Congress, in 1918 and 1919. Five Socialists elected to the New York State Legislature were expelled also just after World War I. And when Communists began electing members to the City Council in New York under the system of proportional representation, the system was abolished, and the Communists were out. With all this, the Communist and Socialist Parties retained a touching faith in the ballot box.

Militants of today have worked very hard in the South registering Negroes to vote, forming the Freedom Democratic Party in Mississippi, the Black Panther Party in Alabama, trying to oust the Mississippi Congressmen from their seats and replace them with black Mississippians. However, this is accompanied by a basic mistrust of politics, and what seems to me, anyway, to be a sharper awareness than was shown in the Thirties of the limitations of parliamentary democracy. The vote, today's radicals know, is only an occasional flicker of democracy in an otherwise elitist system; the voice of the people therefore must be manifested in other ways, by day-to-day activity, by demonstrative action, by a constant politics of protest rather than the traditional politics of the ballot.

The Left of the Thirties had its organized gods: the Soviet Union, the Party, the body of Marxist theory. The Left of today distrusts the crystallization of power in any form which becomes rigid and commanding. Only a few have read Robert Michels, but they seem to instinctively sense his thesis, that there is an "iron law of oligarchy" in any organization, with power flowing toward the top. And so, in both SDS and SNCC, there is distrust of leadership, an anxiety for what is called "participatory democracy," an almost romantic notion that "the people" must decide things for themselves. Hence, SNCC has always emphasized that local people in the towns and hamlets of the Black Belt must be brought along to become the leaders; the SNCC people prod and stimulate and start things, and then move on.

The Old Left was humorless, it is often said, and this is hard to check up on, because historical records tend to squeeze the juices out of the past; but there are enough vestiges of the Old Left around to indicate that this is probably accurate. The Old Left was square. The new radicals are more cool, have more fun, are less Puritanical, less inhibited, more irrelevant. I remember Julian Bond showing me one of his first poems in the early days of the Atlanta student movement, a tiny couplet which went like this:

> *Look at that gal shake that thing;*
> *We can't all be Martin Luther King.*

In the Thirties, Communists and their friends juggled deftly the categories of "just wars" and "unjust wars," using Marxist scripture and analyses from on high to help decide which was which. The Germans, Italians, and Japanese were denounced for their acts of war against helpless peoples. The Russian attack on Finland was justified as a case of self-defense. World War II was unjust and imperialistic until the invasion in June 22, 1941 of the Soviet Union by Hitler; it then became a people's war. It must be said that here the Communists were very much in the modern liberal tradition: both Communists and liberals see war as an extension of the internal benevolence of the system they favor, so that to the Sovietophiles wars waged by the Soviet Union will be *ipso facto*, just, and to American patriots, wars waged by the liberal United States, must by that fact, be wars for freedom. The New Left, on the other hand, is very much influenced by the non-violent approach of the civil rights movement, joined to an ancient American streak of pacifism which goes back to Thoreau and the abolitionist movement. It is not a pure non-violence, as attested by the movement's general approval of the Deacons in the Deep South; and I would guess that if a revolution broke out in South Africa there would be support among the New Left for it, as there has been a good deal of sympathy for the Castro revolution in Cuba. The abolitionists too were not pure in their pacifism; when the war came they decided to support it. I would guess that the distinctions which the New Left makes are, in the first instance (that of the Deacons), between aggressive violence and self-defense; and in the second instance (S. Africa, Cuba, Algeria), between traditional wars for national power and revolutionary uprisings for social goals. I think the strong strain of feeling for the Vietcong in the present conflict stems from the belief that the United States is acting on behalf of its national power, and that the guerrillas in South Vietnam (despite the fact that China may be trying to augment its own power, and Ho Chi Minh his) are themselves conducting a revolutionay war against a foreign invader which manipulates a militaristic, and elitist puppet government.

While most old categories of radical thought do not neatly fit the New Left, I find a cluster of *anarchist* ideas at its core. There is the suspicion of organized power in any form, even the power of radical groups themselves. There is the fear of centralization, and so a tendency for decisions to be made in the field rather than by executive committees; and there is the creation of parallel organizations inside the old structure, as a tiny fire around which people gather to keep warm as a way of *showing*, rather than just talking about, what the future might be like.

Hence the Freedom Parties, the Freedom Schools, the Freedom Houses (radical versions of frat houses, I suppose), the Freedom Labor Union (intended to put the AFL-CIO to shame), the Free University, the Congress of Unrepresented People, and who knows what next.

The militants of the Thirties and those of today have a common ground of concern: the abolition of war, poverty, racial discrimination, and political imprisonment. Both groups looked ultimately to a society where cooperation and affection would replace the scramble for money and power, while leaving the individual free to determine his own way of enjoying life and love. These were marvelously desirable ends. But what the Leftists of the Thirties did was to commit a deadly ethical error: they made absolutes of the means which would be used to achieve these ends. And so they absolutized Marxism, the Party, the Soviet Union, socialism. When the means became absolutes, then immediately the possibility, even the probability appears, that the original ends will be forgotten or distorted. In doing this, the radicals of that day lost the chance to break new ethical ground, and followed the example of other social currents in modern times: a loving Christ-centered religion, absolutized in the church, in ritual, in dogma; liberalism, absolutized in the modern parliamentary, capitalist, jingoistic state; education and intellect absolutized in the Ph.D., the university, the scholarly monograph, and the mass media; the joy of life, absolutized in spectator sports, in television, in credit-cards, first-class passage, and success measured by money income.

The militant Left of the Sixties has so far been fluid and free-wheeling, refusing to deify any nation, any person, any ideological system; and yet holding fast—to the point of prison, defamation, even death—to a core of beliefs about the value of the individual human being. This is not to say there are not lapses, faults, aberrations, irrationalities, pettinesses, absurdities, or that the danger of creating absolutes is not there every moment. And no one can predict what will happen tomorrow.

But right now the New Left to me looks not only concerned, but honest and open, free of icons and gods, full of courage, and very much alive. So, I personally welcome the radicalism of the Sixties. And, while I want always to keep a small thinking part of me outside *any* movement, I am glad to be with it.

Leslie A. Fiedler *is Professor of English at the State University of New York at Buffalo and a distinguished American literary critic. His books include* An End to Innocence, Essays on Culture and Politics, The Art of the Essay, The Second Stone: A Love Story, *and* Waiting for the End.

The Two Memories: Reflections on Writers and Writing in the Thirties

CONSIDERATION of the writing of the Thirties, to me at least, seems not one of those acts of reminiscence and nostalgia which are optional, seems not so much the self-indulgence of a baffled critic looking backward in search of his own youth, but a kind of return to roots and sources in American life and culture which is necessary for the renewal that seems to be beginning now in American literature and culture. It is the re-examination of a past which, to tell the truth, we never quite understood when we were living it—a re-examination out of a sense that unless we understand that past now, the past of the Thirties, we will not come to understand the present or our own surviving selves in the present.

We seem barely to have left behind—and by "we" in this case I mean people in the business of criticizing American literature and culture and the population as a whole—a decade or so which we spent in re-evoking and re-evaluating the Twenties. The years just after World War II, and in our own times, when we were reaching back to the years just after World War I in search of a clue to our own identity in the United States, have been altered as well as illuminated by that search for the Twenties. What we have done stretches all the way from the trivial to the significant. You know we've exhumed the Charleston and certain kinds of dress styles and hairdos. We redeemed the figure of Scott Fitzgerald who was beginning to fade from popular favor and critical esteem. We even brought back into public life for a little while the strange case of Leopold and Loeb, and somehow the climax of the whole thing seems to me to have been that marvellous movie which is a real pastiche of the period, both its legendary gang slayings and its corniest old jokes about "Some Like Them Hot." I think, if we get a monument as witty as that for the Thirties by the time we're through with it, we'll be lucky.

Now, it's the revival of a myth of the Twenties which has helped make possible in the years just before us a kind of new jazz age and a renewal or revival of Bohemian life in America, which has led more recently into such strange developments as pop art, and what we have agreed to call for lack of a better term "camp" in the field of literature and the arts. And, in a way, that turning back to the Twenties has helped us to revive, bring to birth again in America, romanticism—a kind of celebration of feeling over form and a preference of mockery over solemnity. But our hunger for the Twenties seems satiated for the moment and our fantasies demand to be fed with myths of another part of our not-so-distant past, and so we begin to ransack the Thirties. The effort to move into the Thirties has been operating on various fronts, and I think the major way back into the Thirties began as kind of an academic exercise, a whole series of studies and more personal reminiscences. It began with books like Walter Rideout's *The Radical Novel*, or

Daniel Aaron's book, *Writers on the Left,* or a fascinating book
by a man called Allen Guttmann called *The Wound in the
Heart*. But more than those scholarly approaches to the Thirties has been the kind of journalistic account and personal
reminiscence—Mary McCarthy, for instance, digging up her
Thirties' past, and Dwight MacDonald digging up his, and
most recently a book somewhat disappointing but full of inci-
dental rewards, Alfred Kazin's account of growing up in the
Thirties, really an account of making it in the Thirties. And
there are more things to come—I mean one sees promises of
books on the Thirties all the time. I know some of those promises aren't kept. I've been promising myself for five years to
write a book on the Thirties, and probably my remarks here
are as close as I'm going to come to it.

Even more striking to me and significant have been revivals
and reprintings—revivals of the literature of the Thirties and
reprintings of books of the Thirties which have gone out of
print. And let me say at this point that the Thirties which is
being reprinted and revived at the moment is not necessarily
the Thirties that the Thirties themselves thought of as being at
the center of their lives. That is to say, the writers the period
itself preferred—writers like Dos Passos or James T. Farrell or
even John Steinbeck—seem to us now irrelevant and bores,
when they are not just downright bad writers who seem to have
been overestimated because of certain sentimental necessities of
the period in which they first appeared. It's interesting we agree
with the Twenties in their adulation of Fitzgerald, say. We
grant, in effect, that the Twenties understood themselves or at
least they celebrated about themselves what we tend to celebrate now. But I think we're inclined to correct the Thirties
even as we revive them, to instruct the Thirties themselves
retrospectively about their own meaning.

That is why I think we were all so deeply dismayed (I guess
the right word is embarrassed) when the Europeans on the
Nobel Prize Committee, taking that confused period of the

Thirties at its own word and accepting its evaluations, gave a belated Nobel Prize award to John Steinbeck. It's certainly relatively neglected writers of the Thirties who appeal to us now and who constitute for us the real Thirties, judging at least by what we choose to reprint—a really attractive and fascinating little book by James Agee called *Let Us Now Praise Famous Men,* for instance, or the three novels of Daniel Fuchs, or Henry Roth's long neglected *Call It Sleep* which could never sell more than 1200 copies in its own time and which I now see probably in the hands of high school students. I guess the world has a feeling now that they're not only going to read Saul Bellow's *Herzog,* but they want to read the literature that Saul Bellow is reading and that Herzog presumably read in his youth. And what of the great revival of recent years, the revival of Nathanael West, who begins to seem to us more and more the essential spokesman for the period, and the voice which speaks out of the Thirties to whatever remains alive in us survivors of those Thirties, and to whatever is alive in you people who are growing up in the Sixties?

At this moment we're about to get a re-publication of one of the shrillest, most sentimental proletarian novels, so-called, ever written—Mike Gold's *Jews Without Money.* As the publishers begin to realize the Thirties are in, and if they want to sell books, they better get Thirties' books on the stands; but maybe in the revival of books like *Jews Without Money* there is a certain kind of happy condescension. I mean, let's see what they used to enjoy and let's laugh at it, would be like a revival of waiting for Lecky, let's say, on the stage at the present moment. Even books by European authors that most moved the readers of the Depression Generation are getting a new life, too, on the public stands. Not so long ago, the second edition, after twenty-five years, of Silone's *Fontamara,* for instance, came out of revision. And there's a new translation of Céline's great book, *Death on the Installment Plan,* which in a way represents the terror and despair of the Thirties better almost

than any American book. But not only on the highbrow level
and the critical level and the university level, but on the middlebrow level, Clifford Odets comes back to life again in black
face in a production of *Golden Boy,* where all the Jews are
turned into Negroes so that the play can keep up with fashion.
And there is the revival of Humphrey Bogart, as if Bogart's face
was the mythological face of the Thirties looking at us, and the
re-showing of period films like "Grapes of Wrath," or a film I
like much better, "I Was a Fugitive from a Chain Gang." I'll
stay up late any night to see Paul Muni go through that shad-
owy world which we used to think of as a product of realism,
but is a real projection of the Gothic horror which rode the
mind of the Thirties.

And finally, I think the Thirties seem close to us because we
have once again a radical youth movement. Today there's a
group of activist, activist-pacifist, however you say, young people
on the campuses of America who are trying to reach the record
of the Thirties when half a million people went out on campuses in protest against war and took the Oxford Oath swear-
ing they would never bear arms in defense of their country at
the point when they were preparing, of course, secretly in the
depths of their hearts, to do it. But it was a great moment, let
me tell you. And maybe there weren't a half million people
because those were the official figures, but even a couple of
hundred thousand is pretty good. Now we all know on the basis
of what Mr. Zinn has written that there are fundamental differences between the young radicals of the Thirties and the young
radicals of the Sixties. The radicals of the Thirties, Mr. Zinn
wrote, and this was true, were Scholastics, but the word which
didn't occur to him and which occurs to me is that the radicals
of the Sixties are evangelical. In America, you're either a Communist or a Holy Roller, and you pay your money and take
your choice. We went in for Talmudic exegesis, you go in for
holy rolling. In a sentimental way, I like your style better. The
young radicals of the Thirties were influenced by the Bohe-

mian world which existed before them in the Twenties as the radicals of the Sixties are influenced by the Bohemian world which existed before them in the Fifties. And in a sense the radicalism of the Thirties was continuous with the bohemianism of the Twenties as the radicalism of right now is continuous with the bohemianism of a few years ago, and it's quite a different style, that Bohemian style.

The world that the young radicals of the Thirties came out of was a world of bathtub gin, if you were lucky enough. I made it in the early Thirties at the tender age of fifteen. You could boast, you know, standing up here later, that I drank my first drink when Prohibition was still in force. This is a thrill anybody can get nowadays with pop, prohibition of which is still in force, where the discrepancy between the accepted values of the youth group and the official laws of society are just about as discrepant. But all this thinking is that it was gin and the tail end of the Freudian–D. H. Lawrencian sexual revolution which the radicals of the Thirties inherited. The radicalism of right now is identified with the world of hallucinogenic drugs, pop, and other things, and with that kind of homosexual revolt which is so oddly connected with the civil rights' movement, this being a difficult subject that people don't really like to talk about, but that some day has to be brought out into the open and discussed.

The radical of the Thirties tended to think of himself— never mind whether this was true—as a kind of hard Bolshevik, and he thought about violence. The young live in violence and they live especially in that institutionalization of violence which is called the demonstration, which is a satisfaction in itself. I mean it's a kind of society which comes into existence for a moment and has its own real rewards, never mind what it's for. It was true in the Thirties and I presume it's true now. You know the radicals of the Thirties thought of themselves as hard Bolsheviks, and although they took much of the punishment, they dreamed of dishing out some of the punishment, too. That usually never got further than biting the rear ends of the cops' horses and putting a little red pepper in their noses. But the radicals of the Sixties seem to have a different view of themselves, not as the ones who inflict violence but as the ones who are the occasions of violence, the innocent occasions of violence which they suffer. They see themselves as rapees rather than rapists. This is something about the non-violence, the psychological basis of the non-violent movement which intrigues me much.

And then there's another thing which is hard to say to young people, which is that the young demonstrators and radicals of this generation seem to really know all the time that they are indulging in a limited and privileged kind of activity like joining a fraternity or playing on a team which belongs to their youth. And they're going to have it out and then settle down with their degrees and their jobs into becoming precisely the image of their fathers, more like their fathers than it's comfortable for any young person ever to acknowledge that he really has any chance of feeling. In a funny way, that knowledge is planted right there, and I think it's one of the results of the fact that the young are the inheritors, the beneficiaries I'm almost tempted to say, of the cynical wisdom which came out of the Thirties and its tail end.

I think that one can't understand the radicalism of the Sixties without understanding the radicalism of the Thirties because in a funny way young people have a longer memory than their elders are prepared to admit, or than they're even prepared to admit themselves. They have a memory which is as long as the books that they read. And it's this vicarious memory of the young that I'm talking about now. I'm talking about the books which have made the mind of this generation, and which turn out to be, in a very large part, Thirties' books. I was recently the judge in the Dell novel contest, for instance, and the person to whom we gave the prize was a young man named Jeremy Larner who wrote a book called *Drive, He Said,* and although the title comes out of a phrase in a poem by Robert Creeley, the style of the book comes out of Nathanael West. And the style of many of the books which were turned in to the judges in this particular contest were really Thirties' books as far as their techniques are concerned; and certainly the Forties' and Fifties' books, which you people read, were created by writers of an intermediate generation—Saul Bellow, Norman Mailer, Mary McCarthy, James Baldwin—just to name the names that come to the top of my head first, whose own living memories of their own youth is implicated with a radical movement of the Thirties.

And I think maybe at this point in my discussion it's well for me to make what is kind of a central and organizing contention which lies behind it, beyond it, above it, some place in it, at any rate. I think at this point what I would like to say is that the Thirties which the young remember with the help of certain books are not at all the Thirties which are recorded in the official histories or the accounts of political scientists dealing with the Thirties, or fondly recollected by the majority of your parents, or memorialized by the survivors of the New Deal.

What did Will Rogers have to do with the Thirties through which I lived, or what indeed did Franklin D. Roosevelt's First Inaugural Address have to do with it? Let me explain what I mean. There are, mythologically speaking, at least two Thirties. For my purposes, let's say there are two Thirties or two memories of that legendary era of the Thirties, which are not merely different one from the other, but are utterly and totally in opposition to each other. There are two sets of memories of the Thirties which have nothing to do with each other except at some points where they come into conflict. And those of us who walk about the world with one set of memories in our heads about the Thirties find it difficult, almost impossible really, to communicate with those haunted by the other memories or committed to evoking those other memories at all. My own reaction, as I say, to Edward G. Robinson's reading from FDR's

First Inaugural Address was an immediate urge to compose a
counter-anthology of memorable quotations from the Thirties
and one of the things I will do before I'm through with my remarks here is to put before you my counter-anthology.

One view of the Thirties, one memory of the Thirties—and
that's what almost everybody has been talking about, pro, con,
one way or another all the way through—is a mythology, a
mythological memory of the Thirties, which was revived especially with the Kennedy Administration. And one of the influential figures in this whole revival was certainly Arthur
Schlesinger, who seems to be a favorite punching bag of everybody, so I'd better get in my whacks at him, too, before I'm
through. This view of the Thirties thinks of the Thirties as a
period in which we moved from defeat, and if not to victory at
least toward victory; a period in which we conquered fear, in
which we laid down the basis of future prosperity, in which we
prepared for an eventual triumph in a war against fascism.

People who have this view of the Thirties think of them as a
time of the triumph of organized labor, a period of the breakthrough of all sorts of laws and regulations in favor of social
welfare, and perhaps even as the beginning of the emergence of
the welfare state. And some people say at this point "hurray"
and some people say "too bad," but this is a view which most of
the participants in these seminars share. If you have this view of
the Thirties, Franklin Delano Roosevelt is the hero, or if you're
anti-, the villain. Franklin Delano Roosevelt is, for people who
believe in this era, the hero of a kind of euphoric vision of our
not-so-remote past. But this vision of the Thirties—let me say as
a literary man—is embodied in absolutely no distinguished
literature in prose and verse. Only the most ignoble kinds of
middlebrow plays celebrate Roosevelt, and I remember one
other place where he really made it, which was on the pages of
the comic books in the days just at the time of World War II
which always used to have a final panel showing FDR grasping
the hand of Captain America or Superman who's marching off to

help defend our interests against the Nazis and the Fascists. But for distinguished literature, the literature of this period which is preserved in libraries and taught in class, the New Deal scarcely exists at all, and the figure of Roosevelt is irrelevant. If he is evoked at all, it is as a symbol of impotence and irrelevance. Occasionally you find a contemptuous reference or two to the ineffectual legislation of the New Deal in some of the proletarian novels of the period.

I think of a strange book whose name, at least, I want to mention to you. It's called *Marching, Marching* by Clara Weatherwax. Probably nobody has ever heard of it though it won the sole *New Masses* prize for proletarian literature ever given in the middle of the Thirties. It finished proletarian literature, as a matter of fact. Let me be clear about it, the Old Left—the Radical Left of the Thirties—didn't regard the figure of Roosevelt with the violent fear and hatred which was felt toward Roosevelt from the Radical Right. But the Radical Left greeted Roosevelt rather with condescension and mild contempt. I want to give you just two examples because I should like to fix this in your mind, and here begins my counter-anthology.

The first is from a magazine which led a very brief life and was called *Americana,* and I read it because it was one attempt to set up a radical magazine which was not Communist-dominated. In *Americana* it said in 1932: "As for Mr. Roosevelt, personally we consider him a weak and vacillating politician who will be an apt tool in the hands of his powerful backers." But let me call a more potent literary witness to the stand, a man who had only published three stories in the Thirties, but they were reviewed so favorably in Russia that he was considered the rising light of American literature, a man whose play, which was called "Can You Hear Their Voices," was produced under the sponsorship of Howie Flanagan at Vassar College and set the whole Ivy League in an uproar. (Communists were always taking over the Ivy League in those days.)

You may not think of this person as a distinguished author at all, though he was thought of for a while as potentially that. You know him in a totally different context—I mean Whittaker Chambers—who may have arisen into your mind in the pages of a newspaper in relation to something quite different. But here is Whittaker Chambers on the subject of Roosevelt:

> The same strange savagery cropped out in a conversation about Franklin Roosevelt. Hiss' contempt for Franklin Roosevelt as a dabbler in revolution who understood neither revolution nor history was profound. It was a common view of Roosevelt among Communists, which I shared with the rest. But Alger expressed it not only in political terms. He startled me, and deeply shocked my wife, by the obvious pleasure he took in the most simple and brutal references to the President's physical condition as a symbol of the middle-class breakdown.*

Look, this is the Communist allegorized *Lady Chatterley's Lover* of the middle Thirties. Roosevelt is the husband of Lady Chatterley, whose physical paralysis represents the inner paralysis of America. Millars, the happy and potent gardener, is of course the American working class under the leadership of the Communist party, and the lady for whose favors everybody is competing is that working class itself and the heart of America itself.

But so much then for Roosevelt as he existed mythologically in the minds of people at that time. It doesn't matter whether this was actually Hiss' opinion or only what Chambers said Hiss thought. It was the opinion of the Communists in the Thirties and those most influenced by the Communists in the Thirties. And when I say those most influenced by the Communists in the Thirties, this means most writers of first-rate talent then functioning in the United States whether they were survivors of the Twenties just rising to prominence in the Thirties or even fairly young kids who would have to wait until

* Whittaker Chambers, *Witness* (New York, Random House), 1952, copyright by the author.

the Forties and Fifties for recognition. The only considerable group of talented writers that stood outside the sphere of Communist influence were the Southern Agrarians, including John Crowe Ransom, Allen Tate, and Robert Penn Warren, who had issued their own manifesto at the beginning of the Thirties, *I'll Take My Stand*. And to them, too, FDR was an irrelevant interloper representing the hated and feared power of the Northeast, and after the TVA they considered him one of the chief enemies of mankind. I feel obliged at this point to remind you that I'm not telling you something of mere historical or antiquarian interest, but of a literary past which continues into the present, a literary past which you can see in graphic form is connected by an unbroken link to the present.

The two most influential literary journals of the Forties and Fifties, the journals which were the training ground and the first place where young writers were displayed, where the kind of people who are now fast becoming the old men of the literary scene first appear, were the *Kenyon Review,* which was heir to the *Southern Review,* and the *Partisan Review.* But the *Southern Review* was founded by Huey Long, Fascist-mad opponent of the New Deal, and the *Partisan Review* was founded by the Communist party and only moved toward independence when a group of Trotskyites broke away from the Communist party. This is a fascinating aspect of the connection between the radical Thirties and the Forties and Fifties, and through the Forties and Fifties the world of writing in which you live. There's been a lot of discussion in recent years in scholarly books about just how "red" the Red Decade was, but for writers there is no doubt in the world. In the year 1932, 52 or 53 writers issued a statement which was called "Culture and Crisis," in which they expressed total despair over the possibility of society as it existed in the United States surviving, and declared that they would vote for the Communist candidates, Foster and Ford, in the election of that year. I won't repeat the whole list for you, but I want to tell you that included in that list were

Edmund Wilson, Sherwood Anderson, Lincoln Steffens, Langston Hughes, Erskine Caldwell, John Dos Passos, a group who were later joined in the American Writers' Congress, which was the institution organized out of the feelings expressed in the pamphlet "Culture and Crisis." Through the Writers' Congress, there later came into this same orbit Edward Dahlberg, Katherine Anne Porter, Kenneth Burke, James Farrell, Dashiell Hammett, Richard Wright, Theodore Dreiser, and Ernest Hemingway. Add these all together and they look like a kind of honor roll of the literature of the period, or a list made for a course in the literature of the Twenties and Thirties given right now.

And I should tell you that the situation did not change between 1932 and 1936. A poll was taken of the members of the American Writers' Congress, a sample of writers in the American Writers' Congress in 1936, and it came out this way: 36 for Earl Browder, six for Norman Thomas, and only two finks registered a vote for Franklin Delano Roosevelt. What moved American writers, the most sensitive and responsive minds of their generation, to make a commitment which at one and the same time pledged them to social action and cut them out of the main stream of American society itself, pledged them to politics and cut them out of everything that most Americans considered politics to consist of? There were two motives kind of mixed up in the thing, and you can find clues to both of them in their famous statement. One is a kind of self-righteousness, a kind of pharisaical patting-yourself-on-the-back which appears to me to have been only superficial, and anyhow, it appears in all the radical movements wherever they appear. Nobody is more self-righteous than the self-righteous opponents of the self-righteous establishment. Very well, said these writers in 1932, very well, we strike hands with our true comrades, we claim our own, and we reject the disorder, the lunacy spawned by the grabbers. The second thing which was in it—and this is where I want to concentrate most of my attention and what I would like you to most feel somehow before I am through—was a kind of vision of the end of the world, the end of days, the thirteen signs of doom, the pangs of the Messiah, or the absolute blowup of everything. The United States under capitalism, said the statement, is like a house rotting away; the roof leaks, the sills and rafters are crumbling. Not a great triumph of style for a statement written by 52 or 53 great writers, but there it is, and please notice that there is expressed in it not hope but despair, not confidence about the eventual triumph of socialism, but fear.

For American writers ever since the Thirties—and there are, of course, beginnings of this long before in American literature—terror has been the staple item on which prose and verse, novels and poems and dramas have been built. Franklin Roosevelt said the only thing we have to fear is fear itself. The writers of the Thirties said the only thing we have to fear is to stop fearing. To stop fearing is the most terrible thing that can happen to us because, once our terror goes, we will accept the world in which we live, which is an insufficient and imperfect world. What was suggested in this manifesto so sketchily and with such feeble rhetoric, you can find worked out in hundreds of books, poems, stories, and articles written by these very people all through the American Thirties. It might be instructive someday at least for some of you to take a look at the so-called proletarian novels which were chiefly novels about strikes which appeared from the beginning to the middle of the Thirties. I've been reading them through recently and they have been very instructive for me because I've discovered the simple fact that in not a single one of those books are the strikers triumphant. The proletarian literature of the Thirties is about defeated strikes, over and over again. Three of the novels written in the middle Thirties are, as a matter of fact, about lumber strikes in Aberdeen, Washington—strikes which ended with a smashing triumph for the unions, but in the three books the unions are defeated every time. Why? Because what

writers wanted then, what writers needed then, what writers
flourished on then, what they still provide us with when we turn
back to their books, are those images of defeat, failure, destruction, and annihilation, which seem to be so necessary to keep
the balance in the American mind, a mind fed so much official
optimism that it turns to its literature for a kind of compensatory blackness.

I'm not going to read you a passage in my imaginary anthology from any of these proletarian novels, nor will I even bother
to read you anything from that magnificient, terrifying, nihilis-
tic book which is Nathanael West's *Day of the Locust*. I suppose
actually now that I'm here in Southern California, on his home
grounds, I ought to read Nathanael West, but I think I'll abide
by the old principle that in the hangman's house one doesn't
mention the rope. The great causes that moved the Thirties,
you should realize, were chiefly lost causes, local miscarriages of
justice beginning with the Sacco and Vanzetti case. Actually the
Thirties began in 1927, since history doesn't have any respect
for our decimal division of periods at all. In 1927, with the
execution of Sacco and Vanzetti, there began the typical process
of the celebration of victims by the Thirties and also of the
exploitation of those victims by the political parties involved in
the whole thing. And it's fascinating to me that it's with the
case of Sacco and Vanzetti that the Thirties start in the year
1927, because Sacco and Vanzetti in the first place were seen as
martyrs; and in the second place, the whole defense of Sacco
and Vanzetti was based on lies, and the people who organized
the defense were aware of it at the time. Carlo Tresca, a great
American anarchist and one of the organizers of the whole
thing, confided to several people at the end of his life that he
had felt all along that Sacco was probably guilty of the crime as
charged, and recent ballistic re-examination of the gun
owned by Sacco seems to have established this beyond any
doubt. Vanzetti innocent, but victimized to protect Sacco;
Sacco guilty. Let's say it this way: the Thirties begin with

victims whose case is half a lie—half true and half a lie. There were plenty of victims in the Thirties—the Scottsboro boys, Angelo Herndon—they came up every week and one had the feeling that they would be manufactured if they didn't exist; but, alas, they didn't have to be manufactured.

But the great cause of the Thirties, the great lost cause of all times—and it has appalled me that this has not been mentioned in any talk about the Thirties that I've heard so far in these seminars, and it's one of the reasons why I keep thinking that these Thirties are not my Thirties in any sense—was the Civil War in Spain. It's been so oddly ignored so far—this is the great wound in the heart (the phrase is Albert Camus'). He said the war in Spain left a wound in all of our hearts ever since. Deep in the memories of the people with whom I lived and worked in this period that was the war which made for all of us World War II seem like a kind of second-best war against fascism. It came too late. It was too impure. The great war to have been fought would have been the war fought in Spain to defend the Western world against Mussolini and Hitler before they gathered power. This was the war, of course, which Roosevelt refused to support in any way, even insisting on maintaining the embargo against the shipment of arms and supplies to the Loyalist side, which is to say the official government of Spain, though the other side was being supplied by Hitler and Mussolini, but to which thousands of Americans, mostly Communists I would suspect or Communist sympathizers, went secretly anyhow as volunteers to fight in one way or another. This is the war which prompted Ernest Hemingway to write four stories, chiefly bad; a play, utterly terrible; a very ambitious novel, *For Whom the Bell Tolls,* only half good; and to make, I think, the only recorded public address that he ever made in his whole life before either the Second or Third Party Congress. And this is the war which brought even William Faulkner, who seemed completely out of the whole thing, to sign a petition asking for the lifting of the arms embargo, and in one of those little bundles where he disposes of all his characters after the close of his books, made him tell us that Linda Snopes went off to drive an ambulance for the Loyalists in Spain.

The war in Spain was the chief event of the Thirties for most of us, and in James MacGregor Burns' excellent book on Roosevelt it gets one page and a half out of a great, thick, fat book. Nobody knows why Roosevelt did it anyhow. He talked about fearing losing the Catholic vote, but he wasn't always a candid man. The war that seemed to confirm the prophecy of doom that was in the minds of all the considerable writers of the Thirties was the war in Spain, the lost war. A war lost twice over, we realized in our consciousness before we were through; lost to the Fascists who attacked Spain from without because the presumable enemies of fascism were unwilling to fight in time, and already compromised hopelessly from within even before the defeat by the maneuverings of the Communist party of Spain and the Soviet Union acting through them in Spain; a war lost twice on the battlefields of Spain and a kind of capsule version of everything which has happened so far.

But I'm not even going to read you a piece from any of the many books, poems, and stories written on Spain. What I would like to give you is a sense, in the purest form, detached from any causes, any strikes, and political issues, of the despair and terror of the apocalyptic vision of doom which was the essence of the Thirties. I will therefore read you a single quotation, a short one from an almost forgotten book; at least a much neglected book by a writer in general not neglected, by a writer whom nobody on the Left in the Thirties thought of as an ally, or anyone associates now with the radicalism of the Thirties. And I read you this particular passage because in it you can see that the deep despair which really moved the Thirties was only accidentally connected with the Communist movement; that Communism only provided a handy set of formulations for a vision of destruction and apocalypse. The novel I'm talking about is called *Castaway,* and it's written by

James Gould Cozzens. His one good novel, in my opinion, is this one. The Thirties was able to move even Cozzens out of that kind of sluggish iciness and abstraction which obsesses him in most of his books and ruins them.

Castaway is a book whose setting takes place in a Gothic department store in a big American city. There's only one character in the whole book, a single lonely man, who at the beginning of the book finds himself in an absolutely empty but crowded with merchandise department store, which maybe is Macy's and maybe is Gimbel's, but surely is hell. And, as that protagonist moves through the book towards its end, we see clearly that he is intended to be a new Robinson Crusoe. The book is a parable, but this is Robinson Crusoe portrayed at the end rather than at the beginning of an era of independent bourgeois enterprise. You know, if modern capitalism is mythologically invented on the island of the first Robinson Crusoe, this book mythologically tells about its ending. He's a Crusoe in search of a Man Friday whom he can't find, but whom he pursues through the whole book. He finds his footprint on the floor in one place, or thinks he does, and he finally discovers the faithful servant and helper who is trying to help him come to terms with his problem. His essential problem is that with all these goods around him he is incapable of manipulating or using any of the goods which are on the shelves of the store in order to insure his own survival. He's a Crusoe who doesn't know how to live. When he finds this imaginary helpmate whom he pursues through the whole book, he discovers that he is dead and that the man for whom he has looked is only himself. I quote the end of the book:

Mr. Lecky beheld its familiar strangeness—not like a stranger's face, and yet it was no friend's face, nor the face of anyone he had ever met. What this could mean held him, bent closer, questioning in the gloom; and suddenly his hand let go the watch, for Mr. Lecky knew why he had never seen a man with this face. He knew who had been pursued and cruelly killed, who was now dead and would never climb more stairs. He knew why Mr. Lecky could never have for his own the stock of this great store.*

But you know it happened. I mean, when we read this in the Thirties we really thought this was the end. But poor Mr. Lecky, which is to say poor me and my contemporaries, we survived. Roosevelt, as they keep telling us, saved capitalism for us, and the doom which befell us was not the doom we had foreseen, but a doom just as dark in its own way, though one which we had no way at all of imagining from where we stood in the Thirties. The doom which has befallen us is the opposite doom from the one which we saw; that is to say, the world did not end. We have moved on into the Affluent Society. They have turned around and said to us, in effect, the opposite of the end of this story. The kind of government which America has had and the kind of policy which has regulated America ever since the New Deal says to us over and over again that we can have anything we want out of the stock of the great store. More and more and more out of the stock of the great store, but the catastrophe is that, alas, we still do not know how to manipulate or control the goods of the great store for our own survival. All we have been taught is how to want more and more of the goods in the great store of capitalist society. At this we have become very good indeed.

The end for which so many writers in the Thirties so passionately yearned, and for which they feared at the same time because it was absolute ambivalence in regard to it, that end didn't come with a bang or with a whimper. Instead the world went on and on. What happened to the writers who lived in a way that was predicated upon the fact that their world would not survive? One is almost tempted to say that the lucky ones like Nathanael West didn't live out the era in which they wrote—they died in time. Some writers stuttered to silence when the Thirties were over. Henry Roth is a great exam-

* James Gould Cozzens, *Castaway* (New York, Random House) , 1934; copyright 1957–61 by the author.

ple—one magnificent book and then no more. But the saddest thing of all is to see the writers who have survived the wreck of the Thirties because they are in fact ghosts. In the year 1957, I saw within four days of each other on the public platform John Dos Passos and James T. Farrell. Dos Passos was blind, as if history always wants to give us symbols, and maundering on the most amazing concoction and hash of inconsequential ideas that you've ever heard. James T. Farrell only remained conscious and erect because the boys in the Princeton clubs where I saw the two of them appear (that's another joke in the whole thing—Dos Passos and Farrell appearing as ghosts in Princeton) knew enough to switch the whiskey in his glass to water after the second drink. Blind drunk, the ghosts of the Thirties were still struggling on in the world of the present.

And what happened to the writers who were young enough to manage to be reborn again—people who were, say, by the end of the Thirties, under the age of twenty-five, the manuscripts of whose first books sometimes were not finished and most often were not printed? Nobody, for instance, will ever see the first novel of Saul Bellow which was a Thirties' novel because he had to be reborn as a Forties' novelist before he could emerge on the public scene. These reborn men, who were under the age of twenty-five in the Thirties—and again let me refuse to be coy about it, let's say *we* who were under the age of twenty-five by the time the Thirties were over—have lived on into this society and we don't look a bit like ghosts perhaps to any of you because, in a way, we have thriven especially well. We have become professors of sociology, political science, literature; some of us conservative professors of political science, history and literature, some of us liberal professors of the same subject, some of us utterly cynical professors of the same subject; but whether conservative or liberal or cynical, or whether we're not professors at all, but the authors of successful novels or contributors to the *New Yorker*, we've all made it in this society. We've thriven in an affluent society.

And you know, the people who were young in the Thirties have come into the Forties and Fifties with, it seems to me, an extra quantum of energy because we had a demon in us which was left unemployed by the collapse of the politics of the Thirties, and we've been driven by those demons ever since. The society which we had learned to hate and to believe was about to die has added to our confusion by rewarding us; and you know, being human, we not only thrive but we even love thriving. But we cannot love thriving wholeheartedly and we cannot love thriving finally because for those of us who are writers, at least, or critics, or teachers of writing, for those of us who are exposed everyday to the relived literature of the Thirties, for those of us who live continuously with recorded second memory that I talked about today, we're really like Christians after the failure of the Second Coming. We're like people who had a Messianic expectation and lived on into another world. I tell you frankly that in our deepest core we are convinced that this world is dead to us. We don't know whether we are haunting this world or this world is haunting us, but this ongoing world with its depressingly immense and grossly rising national product—gross national product—this only depresses and bewilders us. It seems the absolute and final fantasy which makes the world incredible to us.

We feel ourselves interior exiles and the fact that our exiles are well-furnished exiles in the interior doesn't make a bit of difference. We're like those Communist writers they put in resort houses on the lake in Hungary, with a beautiful boat and all the girls that you want, only you can't write. In some way we can write, but we can't. Well, self-pity is certainly what you don't need from anybody on the public platform and you're not going to get it from me. At any rate, those of us who are in that kind of interior exile feel ourselves profoundly disaffected from everything, still. Those men who have the other memory—the Edward G. Robinson memory, the Moley memory—we feel profoundly, utterly disaffected from everything those men call politics and social action—it doesn't matter to us whether those men I'm talking about be Republicans or Democrats. And I think Viet Nam has revealed recently that the kind of superficial détente between the old writers and intellectuals and the established political community which flourished awhile under the Kennedy Administration, that this never, never truly existed at all. I remember the moment at the invasion of the Bay of Pigs, seeing a young girl carrying a sign on the streets of New York addressed, not to John F. Kennedy, but to his wife saying, "Jacqueline, vous avez perdu vos artistes," but those artists they never had. "Jacqueline, you've lost your artists": does one have to say this in a college community? Yes. And have you seen the almost unwholesome eagerness with which the intellectual and artistic community has swung over to hating Johnson wholeheartedly as if they've come back to their true vocation again? Well, Johnson may not be our friend, and Kennedy may have been a false friend, but we're not alone really, I say hopefully and ritually in front of you, because the memories which I'm talking about—the particular memory of the Thirties which I'm talking about—it turns out has become also a part of the vicarious memories of certain young writers and rebels, too, at the present moment.

And I want to read you for my final quotation—my anthology—a piece of a poem by Allen Ginsberg, who has written a kind of memorial to the memory of the Thirties that I'm talking about, or manual to this special kind of memory, in a poem which was included in *Howl*. That poem's publication in 1956 announced the beginnings not only of a new kind of poetry in the Sixties, but of a new life style in the Sixties and a new kind of metapolitics for the Sixties which underlies the practical politics practiced nowadays. I apologize for not reading all of the poem which has the inevitable and lovely title of simply "America." I apologize for not reading all of the poem because all of it is good, but I do want to read you just the parts that bear on what I'm talking about. And I really don't know whether to give you any footnotes for this poem or not. Tom Mooney is mentioned in the poem—you know Tom Mooney. Sacco and Vanzetti are mentioned in the poem—you know Sacco and Vanzetti. The Scottsboro boys are mentioned in the poem—you know them. What good does it do to anybody to be told that Israel Amter, whose name you will also hear, was one of the leading figures of the Jewish-speaking branch of the Communist party in New York in the Thirties? If you don't know who Mother Bloor is, it will be made sufficiently clear from the context, and Scott Nearing is a great radical figure out of the old American Left whose name at least should be familiar to all of you. There is one Yiddish word in the poem, but Saul Bellow, through Herzog, has taught all of America to feel in Yiddish, so I won't translate the word "mensch" for you.

America when will you be angelic?
When will you be worthy of your million Trotskyites?
America I feel sentimental about the Wobblies.
America I used to be a Communist when I was a kid I'm not sorry.
I smoke marijuana every chance I get.
I sit in my house for days on end and stare at the roses in the closet.
When I go to Chinatown I get drunk and never get laid.
My mind is made up there's going to be trouble.
You should have seen me reading Marx.

America free Tom Mooney
America save the Spanish Loyalists
America Sacco & Vanzetti must not die
America I am the Scottsboro boys
America when I was seven momma took me to Communist Cell
    meetings they sold us garbanzos a handful per ticket a ticket costs
    a nickel and the speeches were free every body was angelic and
    sentimental about the workers it was all so sincere you have no
    idea what a good thing the party was in 1935 Scott Nearing was a
    grand old man a real mensch Mother Bloor made me cry I once
    saw Israel Amter plain. Everybody must have been a spy.
*America you don't really want to go to war.**

* Allen Ginsberg, *Howl, and Other Poems* (San Francisco, City Lights Pocket Bookshop) , copyright 1965 by the author.

It's not the end of the poem. There's a lot more that comes in which he becomes an imaginary Indian and grunts on toward the end, and finally it ends. This is the way the memories of the Thirties worked out now in a beautiful, total ironic dissociation of himself from the established polity, as I've learned to say from the political scientists here, from the radical movements which grew up around it, not in despair and not in apocalyptic anger, but in a beautiful kind of mocking tongue-in-cheek line, "America I'm putting my queer shoulder to the wheel."

Morton J. Frisch *is Professor of Political Science at Northern Illinois University and was Fulbright Professor of Political Science at the University of Stockholm, 1963–64. He has published a series of essays on the statesmanship of Franklin D. Roosevelt in* Ethics *and the* Journal of Politics *which will be included in a book-length study entitled* The Politics of Franklin D. Roosevelt.

The Welfare State as a Departure from the Older Liberalism

THE AMERICAN political tradition is ordinarily understood to have a liberal character, but that part of the tradition represented by Roosevelt and the New Deal is definitely not that of the *older* liberalism. We would suggest that the full measure and meaning of our liberal democratic tradition cannot be understood without having an understanding of the essential changes that have occurred within the framework of that tradition and have altered the course of that tradition. For this purpose, it is helpful to observe that the main thrust of the opposition to the New Deal in the second Roosevelt Administration took the form of opposition within the Congress to crucial pieces of New Deal legislation as, for example, the low-cost housing and slum clearance bill, the wages and hours

[68]

bill, and the government reorganization bill. By examining the views of some of the more outspoken opponents of these measures, we can discern several distinct but related kinds of argument that help to characterize the older liberalism. We are concerned primarily, however, with the way in which FDR's way of looking at questions about the common good marks the limits of the older liberalism by transcending it in the direction of the welfare-state.

As we have indicated, one of the divisive political issues in the 75th Congress was that of low-cost housing and slum clearance. The advocates of the bill believed that the potentialities of individuals could not be realized because of the slums in which they lived, and that putting families in better living quarters and eliminating slums tend to emancipate the initiative and talents of individuals and enable the country to become more prosperous and enlightened. The whole housing and slum clearance program was understood as a nation-building project. But it is impossible to allocate funds from the Federal Treasury, to which the whole country contributes, without spending it in certain parts of the country where some particular individuals and groups would derive particular advantages. As Senator Tydings of Maryland, one of the critics of the bill, stated: "I . . . predict that New York will receive practically all the money that this bill contains. I make the prediction that with this bill in its present form, at least half of the money will find its way into New York City or the immediately surrounding area and that the municipality will not put up a red penny." [1] From this we can understand why Senator Carter Glass of Virginia, another critic of the bill, argued that Congress had no authority to confer economic benefits that were not simultaneously enjoyed by *all* the American people. He demanded to know "upon what recognized theory of government it ever became the business of the National Govern-

[1] *Congressional Record* (75th Congress, 1st session, August 4, 1936), Vol. 81, Pt. 7, p. 8194.

ment here in Washington to tax all the American people to clear up slums in certain specified parts of the country." [2] The characteristic New Deal answer, as stated by the President, was that the improvement of the part was simultaneously the improvement of the whole, for an interdependence existed in the country which made the disease of slums a national concern.[3] In other words, slums and slum housing, while local in their existence, are national in their effects.

The critics of the wages and hours bill saw that the power to be given the wage board in Washington was much more than the power simply to deal with wages and hours. It became, in their view, a power involving life and death over all the industry and all the labor in the country. Behind the opposition to this bill, of course, was the fact that the comparatively low wages upon which Southern industries had been developed so recently could not be raised without forcing many of these industries to the wall and therefore diminishing available opportunities for employment in the South.[4] Senator Walter F. George of Georgia, who in 1938 described himself as a "liberal, but a liberal within the Constitution," denounced the proposed legislation as "bureaucracy run mad" and "the wildest dream that was ever presented to the American Congress." He characterized it as an attempt on the part of sinister Washington cabals to establish centralization in America. "Back of this thing stands the almost undisguised purpose of putting into the hands of a board at Washington all the industry, all the labor

[2] *Congressional Record* (75th Congress, 1st session, August 5, 1937), Vol. 81, Pt. 7, p. 8266.

[3] Roosevelt said (in *The Public Papers and Addresses of Franklin D. Roosevelt,* S. I. Rosenman, comp., 13 vols. [New York, 1938–50], VI, 368–69) that "the United States Government does not remain indifferent to the common life of the American citizens simply because they happen to be found in what we call 'cities.' The sanitation, the education, and housing, the working and living conditions, the economic security—in brief, the general welfare of all—are *American* concerns, insofar as they are within the range of Federal power and responsibility under the Constitution." The italics are mine.

[4] See *Report to the President on Economic Conditions in the South* (Washington, 1938).

in America, with all its political and economic consequences.
. . . [There are unmistakable signs] of an intent to bring under
Washington, with vast power, virtually unrestricted and unrestrained, the great populations in the industrial and commercial centers. . . . I have seen in it the possibility at least of
controlling America through a group of industrial and commercial cities in America, and not the least effective means of
control will be agencies at Washington which possess a power
which never should be vested in any board or any bureau, or
delegated by any Congress." [5] The wage board implements the
task of regulating the economic life of the nation, the reasoning
ran, and therefore contributes to the concentration of power in
the hands of the urban industrial and financial interests, without a concern for the needs of the rest of the country. No
individual or group is wise enough, moreover, to give the rule
for an entire national economy.

The opponents of the government reorganization bill emphasized that giving the President virtual unconditional authority to merge or abolish executive agencies would mean the
increased concentration of power in and the excessive growth of
the administrative or executive branch of the government.
They further argued that this proliferation of bureaucracy, by
implementing the task of regulating economic life, threatens
democracy in that it narrows down the individual's freedom to
manage his own affairs. This is the meaning of Senator Borah's
remark that "bureaucracy is the *disease* of government, and
there is no instance on record in which any government has
ever found a cure for it. It attaches itself to all forms of government. . . . It has greater and more persistent staying power
than government itself. The problem which confronts us is the
restraining and controlling of the remarkable bureaucratic
growth of this country. Burdensome to the taxpayer and destructive of democratic principles, bureaucracy means much

[5] *Congressional Record* (75th Congress, 1st session, July 29, 1937) , Vol. 81, Pt.
7, pp. 7788–89.

more than a casual reading of the proposed bill would indicate." [6] Bureaucracy, as opposed to limited government with
limited powers, was considered to be ultimately incompatible
with democratic government in that it subverts democratic
liberty. As Robert E. Sherwood, the Hopkins biographer, observed: "The cries of 'dictatorship' raised against Roosevelt's
reorganization proposals were much the same as those raised by
the enemies of ratification of the Constitution, except that then
the scare word was 'monarchy.' " [7]

There seem to be three separate arguments here. The first is
that problems like slum surroundings and inadequate housing
are not national problems, and therefore legislation designed to
alleviate these problems does not benefit the country as a whole
but only a part of it. The point of view which guides this
criticism is that the urban sections of the country would become the recipient of the lion's share of governmental spending, and hence would tend to dominate the rural sections. The
second is that the authority granted a wage board in Washington, to deal with wages and hours on a national basis, becomes
a power involving life and death over all the industry and all
the labor in the country, with all its centralizing consequences.
And the third is that the power to rearrange executive agencies
and bureaus, and hence create new ones, tends toward the
dangerous concentration of power in the hands of the executive
and the concomitant growth of an enormous, irresponsible bureaucracy. That the rearrangement of executive agencies and
bureaus would tighten up the loosely organized structure of the
American government is precisely what its critics feared. All
these New Deal measures taken together, in the view of the
older liberalism, have the tendency to produce centralization
and bureaucracy, the diseases of modern democratic govern-

[6] *Congressional Record* (75th Congress, 3rd session, March 28, 1938), Vol. 83,
Pt. 4, p. 4194. The italics are mine.
[7] Robert E. Sherwood, *Roosevelt and Hopkins* (New York, 1948), p. 211.

ment.* Both centralization and bureaucracy were regarded as being incompatible with our traditional decentralized democracy, for, under the circumstances of bureaucratic centralization, government could no longer remain responsive to the will of the electorate. The very existence of democracy itself, as conceived by the older liberalism, was held to depend upon the exemption of certain spheres of economic and social activity from the intrusion of big government.

It is an oversimplification of some convenience to say that the hostility of the older liberalism to the regulatory and welfare measures of the New Deal rested on a narrow understanding of the purposes of government. In a Labor Day statement to the American people in 1937, the President outlined his broadened understanding: "The Government has committed itself to a very definite program in the advancement of the economic, industrial and spiritual welfare of our people. . . . We have attempted to create work security with reasonable wages and humane conditions of employment; to provide better homes and bring the family life of our country new comforts and a greater happiness." [8] We must never forget that an important part of the older liberalism was the simple consideration that all the really important things in life are done by society, setting society apart from government, and that the function of government is primarily to secure the *conditions* of happiness. Perhaps its most important formulation occurs in Tom Paine's *Rights of Man:* "Government is no farther necessary than to supply the few cases to which society and civilization are not conveniently competent; and instances are not wanting to show, that everything that government can usually add thereto,

* Centralization refers to the concentration of power in the national government at the expense of state and local governments; and bureaucracy, as it is understood by the older liberalism, means the further concentration of power in and the excessive growth of the administrative or executive branch of the government.

[8] FDR, *Public Papers and Addresses,* VI, 350.

has been performed by the common interest of society, without government. . . . It is but few general laws that civilized life requires, and these of such common usefulness, that whether they are enforced by the same forms of government or not, the effect will be nearly the same. If we consider what the principles are that first condense men into society, and what the motives that regulate their mutual intercourse afterwards, we shall find, by the time we arrive at what is called government, that nearly the whole of the business [of government] is performed by the natural operation of the parts [of society] upon each other." [9] The older liberalism held especially that government has the function of guaranteeing life, liberty, and the pursuit of happiness, but *not* the enjoyment or possession of happiness. The view that the happiness and well-being of the greater number should be provided for by government is, in modern terms, a welfare-state view, and it emerged in this country in the period of the Great Depression.

Roosevelt was undoubtedly right when he said that "heretofore, Government had merely been called upon to produce the *conditions* within which people could live happily, labor peacefully, and rest secure. Now it was called upon to [raise the standard of living for everyone; to bring luxury within the reach of the humblest . . . and to release everyone from the drudgery of the heaviest manual toil]." [10] He pointed out that "it is a relatively *new thing* in American life to consider what the relationship of Government is to its starving people and its unemployed citizens, and to take steps to fulfill its governmental duties to them. A generation ago people had scarcely given thought to the terms 'social security,' 'minimum wages,' or 'maximum hours.' " [11] The President most assuredly shared the older liberal view as far as it went, but he gave it a *new*

[9] Thomas Paine, *The Rights of Man*, Part II, chapter 1. The italics are mine.
[10] FDR, *Public Papers and Addresses*, I, 747. The italics are mine.
[11] *Ibid.*, IX, 440. The italics are mine.

dimension when he insisted that "all reasonable people must recognize that government was not instituted to serve as a cold public instrument to be called into use after irreparable damage has been done. If we limit government to functions of punishing the criminal after the crimes have been committed, of gathering up the wreckage of society after the devastation of an economic collapse, or of fighting a war that reason might have prevented, then government fails to satisfy those urgent human purposes, which, in essence, gave it its beginning and provide its present justification." [12] The President's statement draws a distinction between preventive and remedial measures, and argues for government acting to forestall, through constructive economic and social measures, rather than always merely to repair the damage.

It was characteristic of the older liberalism that Senator William E. Borah, always an independent, denounced the proposed wages and hours bill as placing all the minimum wage employees in the country under a board at Washington "over which they have no control and against which they can exercise no power. . . . I do not want to place the wage earners of this country under control of a bureau. . . . I am just as much opposed to bureaucracy as I am to dictatorship. I am not nearly so much concerned about dictatorship, which we ordinarily speak of, as I am about bureaucracy. . . . The most burdensome, the most demoralizing system of government on earth is the bureaucratic system of government." [13] Roosevelt's answer to that criticism would be that the securing of economic rights is a crucial requirement of the democratic political condition, and that this implies and requires that "the essential democracy of our Nation and the safety of our people depend not upon the absence of power, but upon lodging it with those whom the

[12] *Ibid.*, IV, 442.
[13] *Congressional Record* (75th Congress, 1st session, May 29, 1935), Vol. 79, Pt. 8, pp. 7795, 7797.

people can continue or change through an honest and free system of elections." [14] For it was the *absence* of power, or rather the unwillingness to exercise governmental power, as Roosevelt contended, that "brought us to the brink of disaster in 1932." [15] The broadening of the sphere of individual rights (that is, the establishment of fair and just conditions in the economic life of the nation) therefore requires the enlargement of the functions of government which the New Deal proposed. That enlargement involved a refurbishing of the older liberalism through the infusion of Hamiltonianism for, under the New Deal, Hamiltonianism necessarily became wedded to a broadened liberal perspective.

It is of particular importance to understand, moreover, that the New Dealers were experimenting with techniques of governmental control over concentrated economic power in contradistinction to the trustbusting solution of the older liberalism. When Senator Burton K. Wheeler, who had been La Follette's running mate in 1924, had led the fight in the Senate in 1935 for the passage of the Public Utility Holding Company Control bill, he had been careful to distinguish that piece of legislation which he was sponsoring, from the NRA which he had opposed. The purpose of the holding company legislation, as he explained it, was to decentralize the few vast overconcentrated national organizations which controlled power plants all over the country. Wheeler believed that it was a necessary exercise of national political power to decentralize concentrated economic power, but the NRA, in his estimation, was an exercise of political power for the purpose of augmenting the economic power of organized industry. [16] FDR furnished a break with that tradition. The older liberalism and the New Dealers shared the view that the concentration of economic

---

[14] FDR, *Public Papers and Addresses*, VI, 2.

[15] *Ibid.*, VI, lxi.

[16] *Congressional Record* (74th Congress, 1st session, May 29, 1935), Vol. 79, Pt. 8, pp. 8399–8400.

power constitutes a threat to democracy, but the older liberalism had similar fears about the concentration of governmental power. Accordingly, the older liberalism sought to decentralize concentrations of economic power, while the New Dealers were more inclined, with some exceptions however, to use regulatory legislation to control such concentrations. The New Dealers, in contradistinction to the older liberalism, viewed a cooperation—not a conflict—between governmental power and private economic power, that is, between politics and private property, but with the political as the controlling element.

The older liberalism could be characterized as follows. The more fundamenal issue of political reconstruction is almost entirely subordinated to the restoration of the old competitive system (i.e., improving private competition or freedom of competition) that would require only a limited government. That liberalism called for the destruction of monopolies and trusts, not their regulation. There was the ill-defined recognition that some regulation was necessary and proper, but no principle was stated. In the New Deal, on the other hand, there was a principle stated that the polity must undertake responsibility for the maintenance and health of the economy as a whole, to the point of re-arranging that economy, if necessary, and re-distributing its benefits. This moves away from an emphasis on the *conditions* of happiness toward an emphasis on the enjoyment or possession of happiness, understood as material happiness or well-being. The welfare state is a polity in which material happiness or well-being is no longer merely privately pursued. The question arises therefore as to whether one should understand this shift in emphasis as a qualitative shift in American politics as opposed, say, to a mere acceleration of political actions, and this question, in turn, raises the further question whether, if qualitative, the change in action was based upon a conscious change in political understanding.

Basil Rauch, a New Deal historian, asks whether the great series of New Deal measures, which included the National

Labor Relations Act, the Social Security Act, and the Fair Labor Standards Act, represent a "new departure" in American political thought and practice. His answer is that "the sheer quantity of governmental reformist activity" initiated by the New Deal produced a "qualitative change" in American government—what is called positive government or the welfare state. Something new enters the tradition, Rauch admits, but it must be understood as derivative from the sheer quantity of reformist activity.[17] The quantitative change, from a certain moment on, becomes a qualitative change, and therefore the New Deal can be reduced to a series of legislative acts initiated by the Roosevelt Administration. This interpretation of the New Deal leads to the consequences that there was no change, truly speaking, that there was only a *fast* deal and not a *new* deal, and that all the fuss raised by the opposition was merely a reaction to the rapidity with which the series of New Deal legislative acts unfolded.

In Rauch, one sees reflections of the notion that the New Deal did unthinkingly what it was driven to do, and that the driving force was the boiling up of events and not the grasp of the significance of those events by FDR, nor the direction given them by New Deal legislation. For to say that the qualitative change that had come about did so by the sheer force of the multiplicity of *ad hoc* responses to immediate problems is simply to say that the New Deal did not know what it was doing. The problem can be formulated as follows: did FDR lead or follow, and if he led, did he really know where he was going? Everyone agrees that he was philosopher-king; he was not a theoretician, but a politician. What we do say is that Rauch reflects the prevalent view that practice makes theory and we, on the other hand, believe that in the case of the New Deal in particular, as well as political events in general, it is the other way around. FDR did not know the deepest roots of, nor could he foresee, the fullest consequences of his political actions. But

[17] Basil Rauch, *The History of the New Deal* (New York, 1963), pp. ix, x.

he did act, and he did know, *in principle,* the character of the change his actions were bringing about. Hence we may conclude that that principle was the directing force of the several legislative acts which made up the New Deal, no matter how clumsy or hasty some of those acts might have been.[18] It is no small evidence of this that FDR gave to the whole a name before any of its parts were cast, for he introduced the term "New Deal" in his acceptance speech for the presidential nomination in July 1932. "I have . . . described the spirit of my program as a 'new deal,' which is plain English for a changed *concept* of the duty and responsibility of Government toward economic life." [19]

Frances Perkins writes that "the pattern [the New Deal] was to assume was not clear or specific in Roosevelt's mind, in the mind of the Democratic party, or in the mind of anyone else taking part in the 1932 campaign." [20] In a campaign speech on progressive government, delivered before FDR was first inaugurated, however, there is a statement of what amounts to an enlargement of the rights of the individual as stated in the Declaration of Independence. It would be possible to suggest that this enlargement (which FDR later called "an economic bill of rights") marks a shift in emphasis, on the level of government, from the conditions of happiness toward happiness itself.[21] The Declaration of Independence defines the rights of individuals in terms of a certain understanding of the relation between happiness and the conditions of happiness. According to that understanding, life, liberty, and the pursuit of happiness constitute the conditions of happiness, and it is the

[18] See FDR's remark to the Congress in 1937 (FDR, *Public Papers and Addresses,* V, 638) that, in his opinion, the NRA's difficulties "arose from the fact that it tried to do too much. For example, it was unwise to expect the same agency to regulate the length of working hours, minimum wages, child labor and collective bargaining on the one hand and the complicated questions of unfair trade practices and business controls on the other."

[19] FDR, *Public Papers and Addresses,* I, 782. The italics are mine.

[20] Frances Perkins, *The Roosevelt I Knew* (New York, 1946) , pp. 166–67.

[21] FDR, *Public Papers and Addresses,* I, 753–55.

function of government to guarantee those conditions, but not happiness itself. FDR, on the other hand, conceives the function of government to be to achieve the happiness of the greater number. He seems to see that happiness as well-being and he defines his own understanding of the change in terms of the movement from political to economic rights. It is *this* fundamental change in emphasis which gives the New Deal its distinctive character as a political movement, for, from now on, government furnishes not only the conditions of happiness, but, to a considerable extent, the enjoyment or possession of material happiness which may properly be called *well-being.** Well-being or welfare is a kind of in-between concept, in between the conditions of happiness and happiness itself. All this would seem to suggest that at least a partial formulation of the changes the New Deal was to bring about was in FDR's mind in advance of the changes themselves. FDR, moreover, was able to articulate what was happening more successfully than any other man of that period.

The particular cause of the transition from traditional democracy to the welfare state, as we've tried to show, is the introduction of a new principle. But Roosevelt, the statesman who introduced the principle, did not consider it a radical change, for there is a sense in which that principle forms a part of the Hamiltonian tradition. The notion that the well-being or welfare of the greater number is to be provided by government is implicit, although we cannot say it was recognized in the Constitution's Preamble, which plainly declares that one purpose of the Constitution is to "promote the general welfare." It could reasonably be argued that the New Deal was in a real sense seeking to carry out that purpose announced in the Preamble, that is, the New Deal's intention of furthering the general welfare, by governmental provision for material well-

* Collective bargaining rights can still be classified as a condition of happiness, but wage and hour guarantees, social security benefits, and living in better residences and neighborhoods are a *part* of material happiness or well-being, as well as being the conditions of other happinesses.

being, could be construed as the pursuit of something stated in the Preamble, deflected perhaps by Roosevelt's turn of mind. That statement of purpose, moreover, is not limited to the Preamble, but is mentioned in the main body of the Constitution—in the clause granting the power to lay and collect taxes. It is a well known fact that the Social Security Act, called the cornerstone of the welfare side of the New Deal program, was based on the taxing power, and approved by the Supreme Court when that tribunal stated in 1937 that Congress may impose taxes to provide for the general welfare.[22] What FDR did, and did deliberately, in our opinion, was to more fully develop and more deeply express that theory stated in the Preamble.

What we have suggested is that liberal democracy cannot reach clarity about itself if it does not possess a coherent and comprehensive understanding of its presuppositions, and make intelligible the character of the *modifications* of its primary understanding of political things which have occurred throughout the course of American history. It suffices here to emphasize only that there was a sudden breakthrough in American political thinking in the Thirties which was accomplished by FDR and the New Deal. As a result of the climactic experience of the Great Depression, and the manner in which that depression was understood, the older liberalism became seriously threatened. What is of immense importance in understanding the politics of the New Deal period is that the controversy between FDR and the older liberalism was not merely constituted by the latter's reaction to the rapidity with which the series of New Deal legislative acts unfolded. It derived ultimately from different understandings of the intents and purposes of democratic government. The contribution which the New Deal made to the American political tradition consisted in its correcting the older liberal view to the extent of correcting its narrowed understanding of the functions of government (or the relation-

[22] *Steward Machine Co.* v. *Davis,* 301 *US* 548 (1937).

ship between polity and economy), and only in this light can
we see the case for FDR and the New Deal in its full dimen-
sions. Fundamental to the welfare state position was Roosevelt's contention that "government has the final responsibility
for the *well-being* of its citizenship," that is, for securing the
material happiness or well-being of its citizens,[23] while the older
liberalism, setting society apart from government, continued to
believe in government as being necessary only under certain
conditions. FDR believed that the ill-being of the greater number was the most serious threat to democratic government and,
given the reality of the Great Depression, wasn't that the ill to
be cured?

Perhaps Roosevelt ought to have perceived that a preference
for the well-being of the greater number does not add up to a
comprehensive view of the good of society or the common good.
On a somewhat higher level (although this would take us
outside the Lockean frame of reference), government would be
concerned with creating a certain moral tone and encouraging
the development of human excellence. FDR never reached that
point, however, for he did not conceive of the function of
government as fostering the development of virtue or human
excellence.* He considered the completion or perfection of the
individual to be outside the framework of government as such,
and was still guided by a rather limited view of happiness. But
while the virtues of individualism as a substitute for human
excellence continued to mean for Roosevelt what it meant for
the tradition, he also knew that individualism was not enough.
It was apparent to him that individual interests do not always

---

[23] FDR, *Public Papers and Addresses*, VII, 14. The italics are mine.

* In a message to the Congress, reviewing the broad objectives and accomplishments of his first year in office, Roosevelt suggested that well-being consisted of
"security for the individual and for the family." [*Ibid.*, III, 288.] About a
year later, in a special press conference for newspaper editors, he defined that
term more broadly to include "more of the good things of life," a greater distribution of wealth in the broader sense of the word, "places to go in the summer-
time—recreation," assurance that one is not going to starve in his old age, and
"a chance to earn a living." [*Ibid.*, IV, 236–37.]

operate in the public interest, and that unrestrained individualism has a natural tendency to turn individuals away from the public or common interest. He would subscribe to the view that the death of democracy occurs when individual interests or supposed individual interests become confused with real or common interests. Considered in this way, the continuous task of the democratic statesman would be to turn individuals in the direction of their common interests or the common good, that is, to establish the proper relation between individual and common interests.

We hope to have shown how FDR's distinctive view of the common good points toward a more fundamental political function for the polity than was implicit in the older liberalism. But this was not accomplished without very great difficulty, as it involved a struggle against the established pattern of older liberal beliefs and attitudes. The essential failure of the older liberalism consisted in a one-sided and over-simplified concentration on individualism and all that this implies for politics and government, and the correction of that view involves the realization that the function of government is more than a mere matter of guaranteeing life, liberty, and the pursuit of happiness, as has been so often supposed in our traditional political thinking. To the extent to which FDR has taught us that a democratic society requires for its preservation and improvement not merely the securing of political freedom on the lowest level, but the guaranteeing of equality of opportunity through governmental provision for economic well-being, he transcends some of the limitations of liberal democracy and even *enlarges* the horizons of liberal democracy.

Frank H. Knight *was the Morton D. Hull Distinguished Service Professor of the Social Sciences and Philosophy at the University of Chicago from 1946 through 1951. He is author of* Risk, Uncertainty and Profit, The Ethics of Competition and Other Essays, The Economic Order and Religion, *and* Freedom and Reform.

The Economic Principles of the New Deal

THE PHRASE, "New Deal" is, or was, a slogan, launched by Franklin D. Roosevelt in his Chicago speech of June 30, 1932, accepting the Democratic party nomination as candidate for the Presidency. It seems to be a hybrid of Theodore Roosevelt's "Square Deal" and Woodrow Wilson's "New Freedom." It came to stand for a group of U. S. Government measures—executive orders, laws and court decisions—over a period in the nation's history. The beginning may be dated from Roosevelt's inauguration, March 4, 1933; its terminal date is more vague. Roosevelt died in April, 1945, but the most crucial and famous New Deal institutions, the "WPA" (Works Projects Administration) —neglecting the "NIRA," soon ended by a Supreme Court decision—was officially terminated in 1943, and many of the measures effected, or at least marked enduring changes. Neither the topic as a whole nor any major aspect of it, can be treated at all adequately in such a paper as this; even the main

[84]

events cannot be chronicled in intelligible sequence, as there never was a concrete program of action.

Discussion of the subject, as worded, could run to indefinite length, or it might be covered in a sentence. The latter would paraphrase a famous treatise on snakes in Ireland: "There are no snakes in Ireland." That is to say that the New Deal policies were mostly political, not economic, for they ignored or defied economic principles. While they were not without precedent in American history, the use of major government policies with political power as the principal motive was undertaken on a scale never before seen in American political life.

There was little that was radically new in this situation, or even in the measures tried by the New Deal for dealing with it. The greatest innovation was surely political, the vast expansion of the power of the federal government, at the expense of the states and, of course, of business units. Even in this field, much had happened in and after the Civil War. Notably Lincoln's use of his power as military commander-in-chief to decree the freeing of the slaves in the seceded states and war-finance measures. This suggests the war measures of the Woodrow Wilson Administration and earlier events; an adequate discussion would call for a survey of monetary history in particular, with emphasis on banking. For in 1933 bank deposits had long been the main effective circulating medium, and it was the collapse of the banking system, crippling the economy, which set the most urgent problem for the new administration.

Besides the immediate task of restoring the banking system, and then curing the Depression, Mr. Roosevelt from the first declared aims of sweeping economic and social reform. His ideals and plans were never very definite, and in fact could not be made so. He also naturally sought power, partly for its own sake in which he was highly successful, as shown by his acts and by two re-elections beyond the previously accepted limit of two four-year terms. (He died early in the fourth.) Yet he did not overtly violate the canons of democratic government, which must be held to justify his acts—for believers in democracy, a commitment assumed in this discussion. (Belief, in the sense stated by Winston Churchill—holding that any other possible system is worse, and nothing should be judged good or bad except in comparison with a possible alternative.) Consideration of the situation in the country on March 4, 1933 calls first for some notice of the immediate historical background, and for looking somewhat further back.

The situation was one of deep economic depression, culminating in an acute monetary panic. It seems strange that the main tradition in economic literature had been so slow in recognizing the need for action against depression except in times of panic, though "hard times" had been familiar in history and literature. Depressions were by no means unprecedented, and action to deal with them was not by any means without precedent either. Measures had, from time to time, been taken by American governments to cope with them. However, in this case, the depression had been especially acute and of long duration due to the preceding war boom. It was especially pronounced in agriculture, partly because of governmental action to meet the needs of the Allies in World War I. The expansion of production had been accompanied with contraction of much debt. Then, because of the inelastic demand for major crops, farm prices declined about half by 1921 (from the 1914 level), and then instead of rising, went down by another third by 1933. At one time in the Twenties, nine counties in Iowa were under martial law, to deal with threats of violence by farmers resisting mortgage foreclosure.

In this country, there had been boom and depression of greater or lesser extent, particularly the long price decline connected with absorption of the "greenback" inflation of the Civil War. This was also especially acute in agriculture, but turned upward about 1896. Serious public attention and a call for action came with the panic of 1907; this did not involve severe depression and was soon healed by action of leading bankers, without governmental intervention, and soon forgotten by businessmen. Various preventive measures followed—or measures so intended. After World War I, the commodity price index, which stood at 69.8 in 1913, rose to 154.5 in 1920 and fell to 95.3 in 1929 and to 48.6 in 1932; farm prices, at 100 in 1910–14, reached 211 in 1920 and fell to 68 in 1932.

By way of historical perspective, the first preventive measure was the Aldrich-Vreeland Act of May, 1908, which provided for emergency currency and established a National Monetary Commission (headed by Sen. N. W. Aldrich) to study banking and currency systems in the U. S. and Europe. Its report (in 1912, under President Taft, elected in 1908) made recommendations, many of which were incorporated with modifications in the *Federal Reserve Act* of December, 1913, under President Wilson. Why this failed its first serious test is a question too complex for discussion in this paper. The Taft Administration continued Theodore Roosevelt's anti-trust policy, and that of Wilson enacted the *Federal Trade Commission Act* of September and the *Clayton Anti-Trust Act* of October, 1914. Anti-trust action began much earlier, chiefly in the states, until the Sherman Act of 1890 gave the federal government jurisdiction. The Interstate Commerce Act, establishing the I.C.C., was enacted in 1887.

Laws favoring "labor" (meaning unions) and "the farmer" were also no innovation. The Clayton Anti-Trust Act—curiously declaring that labor is not a commodity—exempted both labor and farm organizations from procedure under the anti-trust laws, and the Norris-LaGuardia Act of 1932 (under Hoover) forbade court injunctions against union activities. The farm problem had become serious during World War I and the *Federal Farm Loan Act* was passed in July, 1916—followed the next year by the *Smith-Hughes Act* for promoting education in agriculture and the trades. The famous McNary-Haugen bill was introduced into Congress in 1924, finally passed in February, 1927; vetoed by President Coolidge, it was

passed again, but killed by another veto on the eve of the
Hoover-Smith presidential campaign—on grounds of improper
delegation of the taxing power and for other reasons. The
Hoover Administration passed several laws to make credit
more available and provide relief, supposedly free from constitutional or political objections. Perhaps the most important
were the *Agricultural Marketing Act* of June, 1929 (setting up
a Federal Farm Board), establishment of the Reconstruction
Finance Corporation (February, 1932), the *Glass-Steagall Act*
for credit extension (February, 1932), a *Relief and Construc-
tion Act* and *Federal Home Loan Bank Act* (both in July,
1932). No doubt the most important event of the Hoover Administration was the fantastic boom in stocks and the "crash"
of October-November 1929, which had an undetermined part
in causing the general depression and panic that followed.
Some competent students hold that the Federal Reserve System
aggravated the cycle of boom and depression, as it was handled,
or mishandled, by those in charge in the late Twenties and
early Thirties (including the Congress, supposed to represent
the public interest). Now we come to the New Deal and, I
repeat, there were plenty of precedents for action against
depression, but in this case it was an especially acute depression
and monetary panic.

The crux of the crisis situation early in 1933 lay in severe
deflation (decline of prices), and the obvious remedy was to
reverse the process. This called first for restoring confidence in
the banks, so that they could function normally again. In this
detail, the first measures of the new administration seemed
fairly effective, as already noted. How "intelligent" they were,
or how necessary, is more in question, especially in view of
what had happened in 1907–8. And account must be taken of
the combination of pursuing this objective with that of general
reform, in accord with the phrase, the "New Deal"; this came
to the fore when some success was achieved in stopping the
panic and after a little recovery. (Lord Stamp, a recognized

British authority on economics and social policy, remarked on the unwisdom of this combination in a speech in Chicago in the Thirties.) To formulate general promises and win the election, Roosevelt, during the campaign of 1932, enlisted the aid of the celebrated "Brains Trust," including Rexford Tugwell, Raymond Moley, and Adolf Berle. The situation, established soon after the inaugural, was a virtual dictatorship, though based on an election and continued by consent of most of the people at first and without serious opposition during the first year. Even in 1934, in spite of much controversy, the Congressional elections gave Roosevelt's party a substantial gain in both Houses.

It is here impossible and unnecessary to consider or even to list in detail Roosevelt's or his party's campaign promises or the acts of his Administration; the laws passed, the executive orders issued, the agencies set up and administrators appointed—to say nothing of trying to criticize them in economic or politico-economic terms. However, a brief survey does seem called for. The following are a few of the main campaign promises and acts of that Administration.

The day after his inauguration, the President called a special session of the new 73rd Congress for March 9, to deal with the banking crisis, but held it in session to act on unemployment and farm relief. Meanwhile, under World War I legislation, he used executive orders to declare a four-day bank holiday, and forbid exportation of gold and silver or dealings in them without permission of the Treasury. After the election, the crisis had deepened; many thousands of banks had closed and the industrial production index had fallen from 65 to an all-time low of 56. By March 9, a large proportion of the banks had reopened; a return flow of funds to the Treasury and Reserve Banks set in, and within two weeks stock prices rose 15 per cent. An Emergency Banking Relief Act (March 9) confirmed the President's executive orders and gave him vast powers in the field of banking and currency and the precious metals. It also authorized the RFC to buy preferred stock of national banks and trust companies, and the panic was checked. What was lacking for a virtual dictatorship was largely supplied in an amendment to the *Agricultural Adjustment Act,* passed on May 12. The President could inflate the money supply by reducing the gold content of the dollar, ordering free coinage of silver at any chosen ratio to gold, or by issuing paper currency, up to $3 billion. The last two privileges he did not exercise. (One platform promise, repeal of the Prohibition Amendment, had been started toward accomplishment under the Hoover Administration; submitted to the states in February, 1933, the repeal amendment was officially declared ratified in December of the same year.)

Meanwhile, measures for balancing the "normal" government budget were passed on March 20 and 22; and to relieve unemployment, the Civilian Conservation Corps was established, March 31. Reorganized in 1935, it at one time employed 500,000 and, in all, over 2,000,000 by 1942. May 12 also produced the Federal Emergency Relief Act (FERA), granting $500,000 to the states, partly on matching terms. To restore the purchasing power of farmers, the AAA sought to stop surplus production and set up the principle of parity prices on things farmers bought and sold, supported by subsidies. It eased the farm credit situation, providing for refinancing mortgages by the Federal Land Banks (set up in 1916). The dollar was devalued by stages down to $35 per fine ounce of gold, and a Joint Resolution of June 5 annulled all gold clauses in public and private obligations. On May 13th the *Home Owners Refinancing Act* was passed, creating a corporation (HOLC) to refinance mortgages and also make advances for taxes and other special needs; and on May 18, the Tennessee Valley Authority was set up.

June 16, 1933—the last day of the session, called "the Hundred Days"—saw several major departures. The *Glass-Steagall Banking Act* set up the Federal Deposit Insurance Corporation and enlarged the functions of the Federal Reserve Banks, expanded membership of the System, and made other changes. Deposit insurance should prevent severe panics, as long as Federal Reserve notes count as cash, or as government credit is maintained. Beyond this, it has little bearing on the business cycle, specifically depressions. The same day, a new *Farm Credit Act* was passed, and an *Emergency Railroad Transportation Act,* and especially the memorable but ill-fated and unregretted *National Industrial Recovery Act* (NIRA), with its administrative agency, the NRA. This was the "king-pin" of the New Deal, and defiance of axiomatic principles of a free economy was carried about as far as possible; but again, the action was politically democratic. The crux of it was that each "industry," somehow defined, set up a "code" of fair competition, under a self-governing association; on this, "labor" was represented—the famous Section 7-a of the Act guaranteed collective bargaining, and a new *National Labor Board* was set up under Senator Robert F. Wagner. Hugh S. Johnson was over-all administrator of the Act. The objective was to set "fair" prices, fair to enterprises, employees, and consumers. The measure showed some success for a time, but invited monopoly and squeezing of small business, which a Review Board of early 1934 reported as flourishing. Code violations soon developed, until the government was "taken off the hook" when the Supreme Court nullified the Act in May, 1935. One of its titles set up the Public Works Administration (PWA) and created a fund of $3.3 for "pump priming" and unemployment relief.

After the special session adjourned, the fall of 1933 was marked by several actions by executive order. In October the *Commodity Credit Corporation* was set up, with funds for crop loans to farmers, and in November the *Civil Works Administration* for emergency unemployment relief. This was to offset a summer drop in the business revival and mitigate distress over the winter. In the spring of '34, when its functions were transferred to the FERA, it had spent nearly a billion dollars, largely on wages and salaries. In December (1933) the President ordered the Treasury to buy all silver mined in the U. S. in the next four years, at $21\frac{1}{2}$ cents per ounce (25%) above the market price.

The year 1934 was marked by 25 or 30 major new measures or changes in programs or agencies, by law or executive order—too many for listing here. Most were designed to promote monetary inflation and/or extend relief to various needy categories—the farmers, the unemployed, debtors, home-owners, also municipalities (many were bankrupt), and even corporations. Perhaps to be mentioned are June acts establishing the *Securities Exchange Commission* (SEC), the *Federal Communications Commission* (FCC) and *Federal Housing Administration* (FHA), all still functioning now in some form. Also, the *National Labor Relations Board* (NLRB) replaced the National Labor Board of 1933, silver purchases were increased by law, and a *Federal Farm Bankruptcy Act* and a *National Housing Act* were passed. As noted before, the November Congressional elections increased the Democratic majorities in both Houses, and (in accord with the 20th Amendment) the new (74th) Congress met on January 4, 1935. The President's message launched a "second New Deal," asking for sweeping reforms—security against unemployment, old age, illness and dependency, plus slum clearance and a national works program for needy unemployed. The *Emergency Relief Appropriation Act* of April 8 set up the Works Progress Administration (WPA, later called Works Projects Administration); it replaced the FERA of 1933, required a means test, and left direct relief to states and localities. This much-ridiculed institution existed until 1943; it spent about $11 billion on some 1.5 million projects and employed over 8.5 million persons, including artists of all categories. Among a dozen or so innovations of 1935, perhaps most noteworthy are the *Rural Electrification Administration* (REA) on May 11, and the *National Youth Administration* (NYA) on June 26—both by executive order—and the *Social Security Act* of August 14, providing for unemployment compensation and old-age and survivor benefits.

The year 1934 had brought out organized opposition to the Roosevelt Administration, from opposite directions. On the one hand, the "Liberty League" was set up in August; on the other, there were propaganda movements for more extreme reform—by Francis E. Townsend, Senator Huey P. Long, Gerald L. K. Smith, and Charles E. Coughlin. In the face of much criticism, the stormy campaign of 1936 won for the Democrats a nearly two-to-one popular majority in November, and an electoral vote of 523 to 8 over Governor Landon, the Republican candidate; the ratio in the new Senate was nearly four-to-one and in the House three-to-one. Miscellaneous political events of 1938 hardly demand listing; the major event was the President's unsuccessful effort to "pack" the Supreme Court—perhaps counting on the indications of the preceding election. In the fall, a special session of Congress, called to enact a number of further reforms, failed to pass any of the measures submitted.

In the summer of 1937, the country slipped from slow business recovery into a fairly severe recession, and the President's message of January, 1938, asked for sweeping measures to relieve farmers and for general relief and recovery—besides substantial funds for military preparedness. A new *Agricultural Adjustment Act* (February 16) incorporated the principles of "parity" and the "ever-normal granary," and set up a *Federal Crop Insurance Corporation,* and in June, a new *Emergency Relief Appropriation Act* became law. The aim was to reverse the deflationary policy, and new deficit financing did cause some rise in prices. Other major governmental actions during 1937, closely connected with New Deal ideas, were a drastic new *Fair Labor Standards Act* (June 25) and a *National Housing Act* (September 1). The former initiated direct federal control of wages and hours of work, established a minimum wage, and seriously restricted child labor. (Such action by the states had previously been blocked by the Supreme Court, but the new law was finally upheld in a 1941 decision.) Also, the *Food Stamp Plan* was proposed in 1939 and adopted in many cities—but discontinued by World War II and important *Social Security Amendments* were passed in August.

By this time, the President was seeing clouds on the international horizon, and his message of January, 1939 went much further; for the first time asking for no new domestic reforms, his budget of $9 billion included over $1.3 billion for defense. Also not especially connected with the New Deal were extensive plans for federal administrative reorganization—partly put through by executive order when a prohibitory joint resolution failed to pass, and later, by law, in 1940.

The New Deal encountered its first really strong opposition in 1934. By the mid-Thirties the tide of public opinion was already turning. Deficiency appropriations for the WPA requested in June were scaled down by Congress (as again in September) and its operations were further reduced by detailed restrictions and by a strike of WPA workers, causing the dismissal of many. In August, some ten million persons were still unemployed. The outbreak of the war in Europe on September 1 gave a spurt to business activity, reducing the number by ten per cent, and by December the index of industrial production rose from 105 to 125. The President proclaimed neutrality in the war, as required by laws of 1935–37; but a new Act of November 4 repealed the embargo on export of arms, etc., which Roosevelt had opposed. Public sentiment sympathized strongly with Britain and France against Germany and the "Axis," but was "isolationist" toward foreign conflicts, while the President favored action. He was denounced by his enemies for maneuvering the country into war, and he did find legally tolerable ways to give substantial support to the Western allies—until the Japanese attack on Pearl Harbor forced full-scale military, as well as material, participation in the war.

The connection with the New Deal is that it was war demand that ended the Depression, which New Deal measures had failed to do—and soon led to a "boom."

Now I would like to make some general comments on the New Deal. In so far as the issues and acts of the New Deal were "economic," business-cycle theory is the branch of the science that was most relevant in 1932–33. There is wide disagreement among students in this field, where this writer claims no special competence; but as far as known, the Roosevelt Administration did not consult the most eminent economic specialists. Nor did it directly use the main orthodox means of influencing the general level of business—manipulation of the bank-rate; instead this was kept low, favoring inflation, in order to facilitate government borrowing. (The Treasury dominated Federal Reserve policy for some time after the war.) General principles of the cycle are vague on quantities and timing and give little definite guidance on control. The main fact is that price cycles are "natural" where the supply of the object in question changes slowly. A familiar example is the corn-hog cycle in agriculture. When the prices of corn and hogs make breeding profitable, production increases; but time is required for the larger supply to reach the market and depress prices. So, expansion is over-done, and more time is required to work off the excess, causing the contraction in turn to be prolonged and carried too far. (The case of tree-fruits is worse, and with structures or goods of long life, and a lengthy period of production, the tendency may be disastrous for the industry. Such situations call for centralized control, and in a competitive economy private and public agencies provide information services to approximate this result.)

General expansion and contraction of a whole economy is a natural consequence of the relation between the "value of money" (the reciprocal of the general price-level) and the velocity of circulation. To state it over-simply, when business is prosperous, it tends to expand, through increased investment in plant and equipment. The shift of funds and productive capacity away from production for current consumption raises prices in that field, increasing profit margins and stimulating the movement. The price-rise carries back to indirect goods (is in fact multiplied) and is soon projected into expectations for the future. Expansion is financed by an increased velocity of circulation, which appears largely as growth in bank loans and deposits in relation to cash reserves. Bank credit may be viewed as a way of increasing the circulation velocity of "hard" money. Expectation of rising prices makes it preferable to hold wealth in the form of goods rather than "money"—chiefly durable goods. The credit structure becomes strained; and even with no panic or "run" on the banks, expanded productive capacity begins to yield more products, causing falling prices which will reverse the situation, making it more profitable to hold money than (durable) goods, and investment shrinks. In the Thirties, roughly half of the unemployment was in the field of investment goods, which "normally" employed about a fifth of the labor force. For reasons rather obscure, and too complex for an attempt at brief analysis, moving productive capacity out of the investment field is harder and slower than change in the other direction; action needs to be more concerted, less individualistic. Hence, recovery tends to be slow, prolonging the depression phase. Accordingly, it seems to be agreed, cycle-reducing action should work chiefly on the boom phase. But that not only presents difficulty of timing and gauging the amount; public opinion resents action to "kill prosperity."

The relation of this greatly over-simplified theorizing to the New Deal is that the first serious federal government effort to deal with a distress situation seemed to succeed as regards the panic but failed to heal the Depression. The great error of Roosevelt and his advisers was in thinking they knew what to do—especially how to reform economic society, in combination with curing a depression. This "conceit" stands out in many statements made during the campaign of 1932 and later in the

Thirties. In fact, general prices are a very "touchy" matter to deal with. The circulating medium has no "utility" of its own; its use is only to get goods or services from other people. Its total quantity in an economy is immaterial, a mere reflection of general prices which depend on its actual use, specifically on use as a "store of value," at the expense of its primary use as an intermediary in exchanges. The former affects its rate of turnover—changes appearing chiefly in the volume of "credit," particularly bank deposits. But serious interference with men's choice between holding money, in the inclusive sense, and holding real wealth obstructs most of the economic freedoms.

As remarked earlier, one cannot assign dates for the beginning or end of New Deal policies. On the one hand, these merged into war measures for which precedents were present in the Wilson Administration, and back to the Civil War. On the other hand, many of the measures had enduring consequences, good or bad. The problems belong to the economic history of the country, and to its history in general. In fundamental respects, what happened was acceleration of trends which were already in process, especially since the accession of Theodore Roosevelt, and also earlier, in the later decades of the nineteenth century. Finally, as New Deal reforms became post-war orthodoxy, a fundamental shift had occurred between the things for which the market was responsible and the things for which government was responsible. Although the major cause of economic and social change since it became conspicuous has been the progress of science and its application in technology, political and economic ideas have their own peculiar and important consequences.*

* It is particularly hard to know how much to attribute to the New Deal of the vast growth in the power of labor unions—to which a ground-swell in public opinion has given the right to organize monopolies of the widest achievable scope and stop production to enforce their demands, while largely irrationally denouncing business monopoly and acting to curb it. It is widely assumed that employers and investors are the natural enemies of employees and the consuming public. One must think of the establishment of nominally Marxist and "communist" dictatorships in much of the world, and inquire why this happened where it did and not

ADDENDUM

No discussion of the economic principles of the New Deal
can, as I have already said, be purely economic, because the
New Deal was not just economic, it was a political matter. The
truths to be observed are political and philosophical. So, if I
may be permitted to draw a few conclusions in that vein:

1. Social action means political action. That is to some extent
   in the nature of democracy, defined in Lincoln's words as "a
   society conceived in liberty and dedicated to the idea of
   equality."
2. Of course, neither freedom nor equality could be taken as
   absolute. They both need much qualification, as to where
   they are possible or desirable.
3. Theoretical analysis of economic principles starts with the
   individual and the use of given resources to satisfy his given
   wants. This means freedom to make choices in the market
   affected by persuasion.
4. Freedom is empty without power, and serious inequality in
   means limits the effective freedom of the weaker party. Thus
   social justice is finally the question of rightful power relations between persons or between individuals on one hand
   and society, acting through "democratically" chosen agents,
   on the other.
5. All of the things that modern societies have done, acting
   through their governments, affect economic things. There is
   no separating the economic from the political.
6. Strict economic theory must by its abstraction assume complete freedom and ignore the role of government, both in
   law enforcement and law-making. However, the economic
   order cannot possibly function without a legal order, main-

---

in the Western democracies. In the U.S., even the two "socialist" parties (one
near-Marxist) grew in voting strength up to over a million in 1921, and then
receded rapidly, after endorsement of the Progressive ticket of Senator R. M. La
Follette in 1925.

tained by a government and constantly changed to fit new conditions. Freedom has no meaning without some kind of order within which it can function and this order must be maintained by the governmental agency; but the government established to maintain this order is a constant threat to freedom—not in performing its order-keeping role, but in its ever present predilection to intervene in the economy.

7. The economic ideal is instrumental rationality, i.e., efficiency of the social units in using their given means to achieve ends freely chosen. If ends conflict between units, or any are anti-social or judged "bad," greater efficiency means worse results. Thus, the individualistic principle cannot govern in such situations and social action is called for. Social action, of course, means political or governmental action. This is necessary because freedom and equality are necessary —the abstract ideas must prevail within the general limitations of imperfect human nature. Both business enterprise and democratic political life are largely motivated by competition for prestige and power, the latter in large part without regard for any particular use to be made of it. Both organizations have the aspect of competitive sport, perhaps as important as that of a means for satisfying anything that can be called real wants, let alone needs. This game aspect calls for very different social ideals and makes the concept of social justice highly ambiguous. In fact, the ideal of freedom, implying that of progress, intellectual, cultural, economic and political, originating in a "Liberal Revolution" since the Middle Ages, has itself transformed the notion of justice.

8. The *major cause* of economic and social change since it became conspicuous has been the progress of science and its application in technology. This goes back to the late Middle Ages, the Renaissance and "Reformation," when ideals of personal liberty and popular sovereignty began to replace those of conformity and obedience to custom and the authority of political absolutism, after the latter, in turn, had replaced religious authority.

Orme W. Phelps *is Senior Professor of Economics at Clare-mont Men's College. He was a Fulbright Research Fellow in Jamaica in 1957–58 and a Brookings Research Professor, 1962–63. Among his publications are* Introduction to Labor Economics *and* Discipline and Discharge in the Unionized Firm.

The Right to Organize: A Neglected Chapter in American Labor History

HISTORICALLY, the right to organize and bargain collectively is of recent origin and has proved hard to come by. For hundreds of years, "combinations" of workers were prohibited by statute in Britain, and they were classified as illegal conspiracies for the first half century in the United States.* Trade unions are highly sophisticated types of organization, and the trade agreement (the "collective bargain") is an equally sophisticated form of contract, without direct analogy anywhere in the legal world today. Unions appear in economically advanced societies in response to large-scale industrial combines, as offsets to managerial tyranny, with its arbitrary distribution of incomes and unavoidable (sometimes calculated) degrada-

* Every labor history recounts the shift from the conspiracy doctrine of the *Philadelphia Cordwainers Case* (1806) to *Commonwealth* v. *Hunt* in 1842, wherein the doctrine was reversed.

[100]

tion of worker status. As argued by John Mitchell, then president of the United Mine Workers of America, at the turn of the century:

> In its fundamental principle trade unionism is plain and clear and simple. Trade unionism starts from the recognition of the fact that under normal conditions the individual, unorganized workman cannot bargain advantageously with the employer for the sale of his labor. . . . The "individual bargain," or individual contract, between employers and men means that the condition of the worst and lowest man in the industry will be that which the best man must accept. . . . Trade unionism thus recognizes that the destruction of the workingman is the individual bargain, and the salvation of the workingman is the joint, united, or collective bargain.[1]

Most trade-union theorizing has been done by people outside the labor movement as such: professors and revolutionaries. Mitchell's counter-monopoly theory had the distinction of being framed by an experienced labor leader drawing upon his own experience for his premises and conclusions. Being pragmatic and non-ideological (Mitchell expressly denied the conflict of interest between employers and employees which is fundamental to the Marxian class-struggle dogma [2]), the theory fitted the terms of American background and experience. When the Congress of the United States finally faced up to the necessity of protecting the right to organize, it took Mitchell's "inequality of bargaining power" as its basic premise. For over thirty years now, it has been national policy that:

> The inequality of bargaining power between employees who do not possess full freedom of association or actual liberty of contract, and employers who are organized in the corporate or other forms of

[1] *Organized Labor* (Philadelphia: American Book and Bible House, 1903) , pp. 2–4.

[2] "Labor unions are *for* the workman, but *against* no one. . . . There is no necessary hostility between capital and labor . . . broadly considered, the interest of the one is the interest of the other, and the prosperity of the one is the prosperity of the other." p. ix, italics in original.

ownership association substantially burdens . . . commerce, and
tends to aggravate recurrent business depressions, by depressing
wage rates and the purchasing power of wage earners in industry
and by preventing the stabilization of competitive wage rates and
working conditions within and between industries.[3]

However, "the salvation of the workingman" through the
"joint, united, or collective bargain," to use Mitchell's phraseol-
ogy, is only one edge of a two-edged blade which cuts deep on
both sides. The true issue—along with the moral justification
for worker combinations—had been stated forty years earlier
by John Stuart Mill in his essay "On Liberty":

This, then, is the appropriate region of human liberty. It comprises,
first, the inward domain of consciousness (thought, feeling, opinion,
sentiment, expression, publication). . . . Secondly, the principle
requires liberty of tastes and pursuits. . . . Thirdly, from this liberty of each individual, follows the liberty, within the same limits,
*of combination among individuals; freedom to unite, for any pur-
pose not involving harm to others:* the persons combining being
supposed to be of full age, and not forced or deceived.[4]

Since trade unions are organized for the express purpose of
forcing employers to give up a larger share of the product of
industry, and, as a practical matter, frequently involve exclud-
ing non-union men from the workplace, how can they claim to
be exempt from Mill's qualification "not involving harm to
others"? The short answer, of course, is that they cannot and do
not. The unionist's argument has always been that since the
employer is permitted (encouraged) to organize by way of
accumulation of capital, partnership, corporation, or other
forms of association, the workers should have the correlative
right to form associations for the purpose of negotiating the

[3] "Findings and Policies," National Labor Relations Act, 49 Stat. 449 (1935).
The former Wagner Act (as amended) is now Title I of the Taft-Hartley Act.
[4] *On Liberty, Etc.*, The World's Classics, CLXX (London: Oxford University
Press, 1933), p. 18, italics added.

terms of employment or otherwise providing for their own mutual aid and protection.

By 1933, the right to organize had been recognized in this country as a legal abstraction for almost a century—but along with it went the equal freedom of employers to defend themselves against organization. The employers' side of the case has seldom been better stated than in the decision of the U. S. Supreme Court in *Adair* v. *United States,* wherein a Congressional prohibition of yellow-dog (individual-bargaining) contracts on the railways was held unconstitutional:

It was the legal right of the defendant Adair—however unwise such a course might have been—to discharge Coppage because of his being a member of a labor organization, as it was the legal right of Coppage, if he saw fit to do so—however unwise such a course on his part might have been—to quit the service in which he was engaged, because the defendant employed some persons who were not members of a labor organization. *In all such particulars the employer and the employee have equality of right,* and any legislation that disturbs that equality is an arbitrary interference with the liberty of contract which no government can legally justify in a free land.[5]

It was not a unanimous decision, however, and Mr. Justice Holmes deplored the reliance upon "paramount individual rights, secured by the Fifth Amendment" as a basis for striking down the protection Congress had granted union members. "I quite agree," said the learned Justice, "that the question what and how much good labor unions do, is one on which intelligent people may differ . . . but I could not pronounce it unwarranted if Congress should decide that . . . a strong union was for the best interest, not only of the men, but of . . . the country at large." Seven years later, in 1915, dissenting from a similar decision on the same issue (prohibition of yellow-dog contracts, this time by State Law) , Holmes put the matter more

5 208 U. S. 161 (1908) , italics added.

bluntly and at the same time endorsed Mitchell's anti-monopoly theory of organization:

> In present conditions a workman not unnaturally may believe that only by belonging to a union can he secure a contract that shall be fair to him. . . . If that belief, whether right or wrong, may be held by a reasonable man, it seems to me that it may be enforced by law in order to establish the *equality of position* between the parties in which liberty of contract begins.[6]

It was only 18 years from the Coppage decision to the Bank Holiday of March, 1933, but the men and events and the temper of the times had changed. Only three men who took part in the Coppage case were still on the Supreme Court: Van Devanter, McReynolds, and Hughes (who had dissented). Politically, the country had moved from the "New Freedom" of Woodrow Wilson through the "Return to Normalcy" of Harding, Coolidge, and Hoover, and had just overwhelmingly endorsed the "New Deal" of Franklin Roosevelt. When the 73rd Congress—which was Democratic by almost 3 to 1 in the House (310–117), and close to 2 to 1 in the Senate (60–35)—assembled in the Capitol, the question was no longer "whether," but "how" the right to organize was to be protected. The key steps in the progression to such a consensus had been: 1) the decisions and awards of the National War Labor Board of World War I, which were a major factor in the doubling of union membership between 1915 and 1920; 2) the Railway Labor Act of 1926, upheld four years later in *T&NO* v. *Brotherhood of Clerks;* 3) the collapse of the economy into depression and chaos, following the stock-market crash of 1929; and 4) the *Norris-LaGuardia Act* of 1932, which finally closed out the use of the yellow-dog contract and the labor injunction.

   The National War Labor Board—the path-breaking agency in *protecting* the right to organize in this country—was the

[6] *Coppage* v. *Kansas,* 236 U. S. 1 (1915), italics added.

National War Labor Board of World War I, a 12-man tripartite commission, with five members each representing employers and labor, and two representing the public. It was created April 8, 1918 by proclamation of President Wilson, "to settle by mediation and conciliation controversies arising between employers and workers in fields of production necessary for the effective conduct of the war. . . ." The Board sat for 13 months, from April 30, 1918 to May 31, 1919, disposed of 1,245 "controversies," and although it had no legal authority to enforce its decisions, got a high degree of compliance with its awards. Perhaps its most influential finding was the statement of principles upon which its decisions were to be based. Rule No. 2 was the key; it might have been written by Gompers himself:

The right of workers to organize in trade unions and to bargain collectively through chosen representatives is recognized and affirmed. This right shall not be denied, abridged, or interfered with by the employers in any manner whatsoever. . . .

Employers should not discharge workers for membership in trade unions, nor for legitimate trade-union activities.[7]

In its awards the Board showed that the rule meant what it said. In case after case after case, employers were forbidden to discriminate against workers for union activity; discharged employees were ordered reinstated with back pay; the blacklisting of union men was proscribed; company unions or employee representation plans were held no bar to membership in bona fide labor organizations; and it was pronounced the duty of employers to recognize and deal with committees of their employees once they had been constituted. A portion of the Brooklyn Rapid Transit System decision of October 24, 1918, illustrates the Board's thinking:

[7] *Report of the Secretary of the National War Labor Board* (Washington: U. S. Government Printing Office, 1920) , pp. 52–53.

The right of the workers of this company freely to organize in trade unions, or to join the same, and to bargain collectively, is affirmed, and discharges for legitimate union activities, interrogation of workers by officials as to their union affiliations, espionage by agents or representatives of the company, visits by officials of the company to the neighborhood of the meeting place of the organization for the purpose of observing the men who belong to such unions, to their detriment as employees of the company, and like actions, the intent of which is to discourage and prevent men from exercising the right of organization, must be deemed an interference with their rights as laid down in the principles of the board.[8]

The encouraging effect of this form of protection was immediately apparent in the statistics of union membership, which rose from 2,976,000 in 1917 to 4,046,000 in 1919 and reached a high point of 5,034,000 in 1920. Termination of the war emergency (and of the Board's activity) was followed in the Twenties by a violent anti-union reaction in American industry, institution of the open-shop "American Plan," and coordination of strikebreaking, blacklisting, and labor espionage upon a broad scale which was uncovered by the La Follette Committee a decade later.[9] Union membership fell almost as fast as it had risen previously; within three years it was down to 3,549,000.

Then, at what would seem to be one of the most unlikely points in the history of labor relations in the United States— halfway through President Coolidge's second term—Congress passed its first really modern labor law, the *Railway Labor Act of 1926*.[10] The prime distinguishing features of this legislation

[8] *Ibid.*, p. 55.

[9] See *Violations of Free Speech and Rights of Labor*, Report of the Committee on Education and Labor, "Industrial Espionage," U. S. Senate, Report No. 46, Part 3, 75th Congress, 2d session (Washington: U. S. Government Printing Office, 1938).

[10] 44 Stat. 577. One explanation: it was the first labor law that union representatives had been invited to help draft. The key individual here was Donald R. Richberg, then counsel to the Railway Labor Executives Association.

were two: first, the major premise of the National War Labor Board (World War I) was given statutory sanction:

Employees shall have the right to organize and bargain collectively through representatives of their own choosing. . . . No carrier, its officers or agents, shall deny or in any way question the right of its employees to join, organize, or assist in organizing the labor organization of their choice, and it shall be unlawful for any carrier to interfere in any way with the organization of its employees, or to use the funds of the carrier in maintaining or assisting or contributing to any labor organization . . . or to influence or coerce employees in an effort to induce them to join or not to join or remain members of any labor organization. . . .

Second, the above guarantee was supported by the creation of a professional, full-time administrative agency, a "Board of Mediation," to interpret and administer the statute and assist in settling disputes, with authority to intervene at the request of either party or on its own motion.*

The law was soon tested by the Brotherhood of Railway and Steamship Clerks, Freight Handlers, and Express and Station Employees, which in 1927 sought to enjoin the Texas and New Orleans Railway from intimidating its members and forcing them to leave the union and join a "system association" created by the company. Three years later, in one of the landmark labor opinions of the U. S. Supreme Court, Chief Justice Hughes and a unanimous Court laid to rest the Adair and Coppage decisions and returned to the principles of Holmes and Mitchell:

We entertain no doubt of the constitutional authority of Congress to enact the prohibition. . . . The petitioners invoke the principle declared in *Adair* v. *U. S.* . . . and *Coppage* v. *Kansas* . . . but

* A third distinction of the act, unimportant in this context but indicative of the law's sophistication was its classification of disputes by categories and provision for different methods of adjusting each.

these decisions are inapplicable. The . . . Act of 1926 does not interfere with the normal exercise of the right of the carrier to select its employees or to discharge them. The statute is not aimed at this right of the employers but at the interference with the right of employees to have representatives of their own choosing.[11]

The T&NO decision came in 1930, the first year of the Great Depression. In that year (we now know) unemployment averaged 8.7 per cent; the rate was not to go below 9 per cent again on an annual basis for twelve long years, until the wartime year of 1942. By 1933, one out of every four persons in the labor force was desperately looking for work. Literally millions of families had lost jobs, incomes, savings, homes, possessions, and self-respect. But above all, they had lost confidence in the American business system and the men running it.[12] To the army of jobless industrial workers, laid off after years of service with no chance of recall, self-organization and collective bargaining at least offered hope, and a few alert labor leaders—John L. Lewis, Sidney Hillman, David Dubinsky, all of them heading up big industrial unions—set about reviving their own organizations and planning organizing drives in the open-shop mass-production industries of the country. The success they met with is now history—the history of the CIO and eventually of a reformed American Federation of Labor.[13] Through the middle 1930's trade unionism was a true grass-roots movement; day after day, union offices were overwhelmed by appeals to send out organizers who could show groups of workers how to form and run a union.

No defense weapon used by employers to stop labor organization was more detested by trade unionists than the iniquitous combination of the yellow-dog contract and the labor injunc-

---

[11] *T&NO Railway* v. *Brotherhood of Clerks*, 281 U. S. 548 (1930) .

[12] See Arthur M. Schlesinger, Jr., *The Crisis of the Old Order*, Volume I of *The Age of Roosevelt* (New York: The Macmillan Company, 1956) , Chapter 1.

[13] The story recounted in Walter Galenson's *The CIO challenge to the AFL, a History of the American Labor Movement, 1935–1941* (Cambridge: Harvard University Press, 1960) .

tion. Upheld by Supreme Court decision as constitutionally impregnable in the Adair and Coppage cases, and finally grounded in common law in *Hitchman Coal & Coke Co.* v. *Mitchell*,[14] the two instruments combined: 1) dubious legality (of individual-bargaining contracts), 2) criminal penalties (for contempt of court where restraining orders were disregarded), and 3) often *ex parte* proceedings before "injunction judges," with the union unrepresented in court.[15] Sections 6 and 20 of the *Clayton Act* of 1914 had been designed to exempt unions from restraining orders, but the (seemingly) plain intent of the law was neutralized by judicial decision in a series of Supreme Court decisions of the Twenties.[16]

In 1932, with twelve million men and women out of work, a liberal Senator (George Norris of Nebraska) and a liberal Congressman (Fiorella La Guardia of New York) teamed up to frame a statute which declared that the individual-bargaining (yellow-dog) contract was "in conflict with . . . public policy . . . (and) shall not be enforceable in any court of the United States and shall not afford any basis for the granting of legal or equitable relief by any such court" of the United States, and hedged the labor injunction with so many safeguards as to make its use thereafter impracticable.[17]

It took four years to bring to a conclusion the campaign to establish a legal basis for the protection of the right to organize and bargain collectively: from June 16, 1933, which is the date of passage of the *National Industrial Recovery Act*,[18] with its crucial and controversial Section 7a, to April 12, 1937, when a

---

[14] 243 U. S. 332 (1917), with Holmes, Brandeis, and Clark dissenting.

[15] Cf. Felix Frankfurter and N. Greene, *The Labor Injunction* (New York: The Macmillan Company, 1930), and E. E. Witte, *The Government in Labor Disputes* (New York: McGraw-Hill Book Co., Inc., 1932).

[16] *Duplex Printing Press Co.* v. *Deering*, 254 U. S. 443 (1921): *American Steel Foundries* v. *Tri-City Central Trades Council*, 257 U. S. 184 (1921); *Truax* v. *Corrigan*, 257 U. S. 312 (1921), and *Bedford Cut Stone Co.* v. *Journeymen Stone Cutters' Association of North America, et. al.*, 274 U. S. 37 (1927).

[17] 47 Stat. 70.

[18] 48 Stat. 214.

divided court shocked the business world by upholding the
constitutionality of the *Wagner Act* and simultaneously breaking open the straitjacket of the commerce clause, in *National
Labor Relations Board* versus *Jones & Laughlin Steel Corporation*.[19] The entire period was one of turmoil, confusion, experimentation, and violent disagreement, as reflected by the following calendar:

1. June 16, 1933: passage of the *National Industrial Recovery Act*
2. August 5, 1933 (7 weeks later) : establishment of the National Labor Board to adjudicate disputes arising under
   Section 7a of the codes of fair competition
3. December 16, 1933 (4 months later) : official approval of
   the National Labor Board by the President in Executive Order No. 6511, subsequently amended twice in
   E.O. 6580 (February 1, 1934) and E.O. 6612-A (February 23, 1934)
4. July 9, 1934 (7 months later) : creation of the (1st) National Labor Relations Board, vice the NLB, under
   authority of Public Resolution No. 44 [20]
5. May 27, 1935 (10 months later) : the NIRA held unconstitutional in *Schechter Corporation* versus *U. S.*,[21] and the
   disappearance with it of Section 7a and the authority of
   the (1st) National Labor Relations Board
6. July 5, 1935 (6 weeks later) : passage of the *National
   Labor Relations (Wagner) Act,* giving independent
   statutory authority to the NLRB [22]
7. April 12, 1937 (21 months later) : *NLRB* versus *Jones &
   Laughlin*

[19] 301 U. S. 1 (1937).
[20] 48 Stat. 1183.
[21] 295 U. S. 495.
[22] 49 Stat. 449.

Few public issues in this century have excited more heated controversy than Section 7a of the *National Industrial Recovery Act,* from which the present national labor policy is directly descended. The key provisions were:

> Every code of fair competition . . . shall contain the following conditions: (1) That employees shall have the right to organize and bargain collectively through representatives of their own choosing, and shall be free from the interference, restraint, or coercion of employers of labor, or their agents, in the designation of such representatives or in self-organization or in other concerted activities for the purpose of collective bargaining or other mutual aid or protection; (2) that no employee and no one seeking employment shall be required as a condition of employment to join any company union or to refrain from joining, organizing, or assisting a labor organization of his own choosing. . . .*

The above conditions precedent to the acquisition of a Blue Eagle (which showed that an employer had signed the President's Reemployment Agreement and was eligible for the privileges associated with the codes of fair competition) set off what *Fortune* called, four and a half years later,[23] "a major labor upheaval, which can fairly be described as one of the greatest mass movements in our history."

To union leaders, it was an invitation to start signing up new members in the coal mines, in textiles and clothing manufacture, but especially in the open-shop, mass-production, metalworking industries led by the big automobile firms and the producers of iron and steel. To many employers, forgetful (or fearful) of the brief lesson taught by the National War Labor Board of World War I, "self-organization for the purpose of collective bargaining" meant company unions (employee representation plans), designed by management, installed by

---

* A third subsection dealt with maximum hours, minimum wages, etc. It was relatively noncontroversial, at least in comparison with the above.

[23] "The Industrial War," *Fortune,* November, 1937, p. 105 ff.

superintendents and foremen—the membership restricted to plant personnel with no "outside" representatives. It also meant a simultaneous full-scale attack upon independent union organizers ("labor agitators"), both within and outside the plant, by means of labor spies, blacklisting, discharge and discrimination, refusal of free elections, and refusal to deal with certified union representatives. Eventually—after passage of the *Wagner Act*—these attitudes settled in some cases into deliberate noncompliance with the Federal law, upon advice of counsel, on grounds that the statute was unconstitutional.

For employers interested in the organization of company unions, there was soon a pair of manuals: *Labor Relations under the Recovery Act,* by Ordway Tead and Henry C. Metcalf,[24] two prominent authorities on personnel practices and procedure, and the National Industrial Conference Board's *Collective Bargaining through Employee Representation Plans,*[25] both printed in 1933. When, in 1935, the Bureau of Labor Statistics conducted a sample survey of approximately 600 firms with company unions, it found that 64 per cent of the plans, covering 58 per cent of the workers, had been installed during the NRA period, 1933–35.[26]

The slow but definite progress of governmental protection of the right to organize may be traced in the composition, functions, and legal basis of the agencies created for the purpose during the four-year period 1933–37. In all, three boards were set up to administer the law: the first two—the National Labor

[24] NY: McGraw-Hill Book Co., Inc., 1933. Tead and Metcalf were already well known as co-authors of one of the first textbooks on personnel management, *Personnel Administration: Its Principles and Practices,* which appeared in a third edition during 1933. *Labor Relations under the Recovery Act* was intended "to supply practical aid to trade associations and to employers concerning improved methods of conducting their labor relations. . . . To this end Chaps. II, III, and IV will be concerned with . . . ways and means of introducing some plan of employee representation." Preface, v–vi.

[25] New York: National Industrial Conference Board, 1933.

[26] *Monthly Labor Review,* October, 1935, p. 867.

Board and the (1st) National Labor Relations Board—under authority of Section 7a of the NIRA, and the third, the National Labor Relations Board of the *Wagner Act.* The National Labor Board was created informally (but with the approval of President Roosevelt), upon recommendation of the Industrial Advisory Board and the Labor Advisory Board of the National Recovery Administration. Its job was to "consider, adjust and settle differences and controversies that may arise through differing interpretations of the President's Reemployment Agreement"; [27] in a word, to mediate disputes which were getting out of hand. It was a non-salaried, part-time, tripartite body, with three labor and three industry members, plus an impartial (public) chairman. It had no authority, no instructions (apart from the above), and no powers of enforcement. Four months *after* its creation, it was formalized by the President in Executive Order No. 6511, and two subsequent Executive Orders ratified its work and strengthened its legal base, but in the turbulent atmosphere of the early New Deal it was already on the way out.

The (1st) National Labor Relations Board came on the scene as the successor to the NLB. It was a wholly different type of agency, with three full-time, paid, professional members, one of whom served as chairman.* Building on the experience of the National Labor Board, Congress (in Public Resolution N. 44) empowered it to investigate disputes, issue rules and regulations, conduct elections, hold hearings and issue findings of fact, and, upon request, to act as a board of arbitration; all of these things the NLB had found necessary to do, but without prior authorization and relying only on the uncertain support of the National Recovery Administration, which was fre-

---

[27] *Decisions of the National Labor Board August 1933–March 1934* (Washington: U. S. Government Printing Office, 1934), p. v.

* Board personnel consisted of Prof. Harry A. Millis (University of Chicago), Mr. Edwin S. Smith, and Dean Lloyd K. Garrison (Law School of the University of Wisconsin).

quently in hot water itself. For elections of union representatives only, the (1st) NLRB had the power to subpoena witnesses, take testimony under oath, and issue orders enforceable by the courts. This was a clear step forward, but the reorganization stopped short at the boundaries of the District of Columbia. The nationwide regional organization remained that of the NLB. Cases were heard before tripartite panels of labor, industry, and public members; the function of the regional directors and their associates was still mediation. Only as a last resort were cases to be referred to Washington for hearing and settlement.[28]

Board No. 3 was the National Labor Relations Board of the *Wagner Act,* a three-man, paid, professional administrative commission, with an independent statutory base, instructions, authority, and full powers of enforcement. Its regional staff was the same—professional, paid, full-time. It was instructed in the statute *not* to employ mediators or conciliators.* In sum, Congress decided that protection of the right to organize and bargain collectively was not a matter of *mediating the interests* of the parties, but of *protecting the rights* of one of the parties—the workers.

Protection of the right to organize, however, turned out to be a matter of limiting the discretion of employers in areas where they were accustomed to exercising a free hand. It was the National Labor Board—an unofficial, part-time, "amateur" body, without statutory authority or powers of investigation or enforcement—that laid down the ground rules which became the jurisprudence of its successors. In the process it soon switched its emphasis from the mediation of disputes (over wages, hours, and conditions of employment) to quasi-judicial interpretation of the statute. Here its decisions became prece-

---

[28] Lewis L. Lorwin and Arthur Wubnig, *Labor Relations Boards* (Washington: The Brookings Institution, 1935) , pp. 296–7.
* When these were available from the staff of the Department of Labor.

dent-setting and eventually enabled Senator Wagner (the chairman) and his colleagues to block out the key areas of employer violation of the rights of workers which became the unfair labor practices of the *National Labor Relations Act* of 1935.

The National Labor Board is a neglected chapter in the history of American labor relations, its achievements generally passed over by historians of the New Deal in favor of the work of subsequent labor relations boards, just as its accomplishments at the time were overshadowed by the pyrotechnics of General Hugh Johnson, Administrator of the Blue Eagle, and his articulate general counsel, Donald R. Richberg. Nevertheless, the NLB was a remarkable body, its performance one of the outstanding contributions of the period. It was chaired by Senator Robert F. Wagner, an experienced legislator, jurist, and former lieutenant-governor of the State of New York, already (at the beginning of his second term) an influential member of the U. S. Senate, who has the credit for initiating three of the most important bills of the time: *the National Industrial Recovery Act,* the *National Labor Relations Act,* and the *Social Security Act.*

The industry and labor members were equally prominent. Employers were represented by: Walter C. Teagle, president of Standard Oil Co. of New Jersey and chairman of the Industrial Advisory Board of the National Recovery Administration; Gerard Swope, president of General Electric Co. and member of the Industrial Advisory Board; and Louis E. Kirstein, vice-president, Wm. Filene's Sons Co. of Boston. All had long records of public and community service extending back to World War I days and beyond. On the labor side were: Leo Wolman, professor of economics at Columbia University, chairman of the Labor Advisory Board of NRA, and a former research director for the Amalgamated Clothing Workers of America; William Green, president of the American Federation of

Labor, member of the Labor Advisory Board (NRA); and John L. Lewis, president of the United Mine Workers of America and also a member of the Labor Advisory Board.*

These were all busy men, with full-time obligations to the organizations they headed or the positions they occupied elsewhere. Much of the real work of the Board was done by its extremely able executive secretary, William M. Leiserson, one of the best-informed labor relations experts in the country.

Leiserson, an immigrant from Estonia at the age of seven, studied economics at the University of Wisconsin under John R. Commons, taking a Ph.D. at Columbia. He then became an expert on unemployment in New York State, served as deputy industrial commissioner for the State of Wisconsin for three years, directed the research of the U. S. Commission on Industrial Relations in 1914–15, was chief of the division of labor administration in the U. S. Department of Labor during World War I, and spent seven years as chairman of various boards of arbitration in the clothing industry of Rochester, New York City, Baltimore, and Chicago. From 1927 to 1934 he was professor of economics at Antioch College. Few people knew industrial relations better than he, either theoretically or at first hand. In New York, he had known and worked with the then State Senator Robert Wagner, chairman of the New York State Factory Investigating Commission. In Washington during World War I, he had met and dealt with Swope and Kirstein,

* On March 3, 1934, the Board was reorganized with the addition of two vice-chairmen— (Samuel) Clay Williams for industry (president, R. J. Reynolds Tobacco Co.) and Leon C. Marshall for labor (political economist, professor in the Institute of Law, Johns Hopkins University) —and an increase of industry and labor members to five each. The final line-up was: Industry—Henry S. Dennison (Dennison Mfg. Co.), Ernest Draper (Hills Bros. Co., food products), Pierre S. du Pont (E. I. du Pont de Nemours & Co.), Kirstein, and Teagle; Labor—George L. Berry (president, International Pressmen and Assistants Union), Green, Francis J. Haas (president, National Catholic School of Social Service), Lewis, and Wolman. *Decisions of the National Labor Board, August 1933–March 1934* (cited hereafter as *Decisions 1933–34*), p. iii. By the time of the reorganization, the Board had registered most of its important decisions and was near collapse from contradictory opinions by NRA administrators, undercutting by the President, and flat defiance by several prominent industrialists.

both of whom were purchasing agents for the government. As arbitrator in the clothing industry, he knew intimately Leo Wolman, research director for the Clothing Workers. It was primarily due to Leiserson's knowledge, energy, and administrative skill that the NLB was able to move so rapidly into the widening gap between the promise and realization of Section 7a.*

In its first case, decided less than a week after the Board was appointed, the NLB settled a primary issue—representation— with the so-called "Reading Formula"; a procedure which is, in all major respects, still in effect as standard practice of the National Labor Relations Board. The problem was a major strike of hosiery workers for recognition in the mills in Berks County, Pennsylvania, with Reading as the key location. Ruling, first, that the strike must end and all strikers be returned to work without prejudice or discrimination, the Board laid down the principle of free elections for the purpose of designating representatives for collective bargaining. It specified:

1) advance notice of the time and place of the election;

2) voting by secret ballot under NLB supervision;

3) all workers on the payroll at the time of strike, but none hired thereafter, eligible to vote; and

4) the representatives so chosen authorized to negotiate with the employer in working out agreements covering wages, hours, and working conditions.[29]

The critical question of what constitutes a majority (of those voting and not of those eligible to vote) was answered in the

* Leiserson's subsequent career was a series of important contributions to labor relations. He was chairman of the National Mediation Board (Railway Labor Act) from 1934 to 1939, member of the NLRB from 1939 to 1943, lecturer and visiting professor at various universities, and an independent arbitrator and labor relations consultant until his death in 1957. In 1938 he summed up the experience of a quarter of a century in *Right and Wrong in Labor Relations* (Berkeley: University of California Press, 1938).

[29] *NRA Release No. 285,* August 11, 1933, in Lorwin and Wubnig, pp. 96–98. As the "formula" was in reality a rule, the decision was not reported in *Decisions 1933–34.*

Denver Tramway Corporation case, March 1, 1934,[30] in a manner subsequently upheld by the U. S. Supreme Court in *New
York Handkerchief Manufacturing Co.* versus *NLRB*.[31]

In a series of decisions, the Board held that workers could not
be restricted to fellow employees in their choice of representatives,[32] that they could be represented by organizations (unions)
as well as by individuals,[33] laid down the ground rules for deciding claims of discriminatory discharge,[34] and distinguished
between invalid (employer-dominated, or "imposed") and
valid (free choice of workers) company unions.

In view of employer activity in setting up employee representation plans, the status of company unions was the key issue to
come before the Board.[35] In the National Lock Company case,
decided February 21, 1934 (it had been pending since a strike
was called in August, 1933), the Board described a procedure
which had become almost standard practice in some of the
heavy industries: [36]

An election was held within the plant for the choice of employee
representatives on October 3rd. This plan was promulgated by the
company and was explained to the employees less than an hour
before the election. A meeting of the employees in each department

[30] *Decisions 1933–34*, pp. 64–65.

[31] 311 U. S. 704 (1941).

[32] Berkeley Woolen Mills, September 6, 1933, *Decisions 1933–34*, pp. 5–6.

[33] Hall Baking Co., March 8, 1934, pp. 83–84.

[34] See Transcontinental and Western Air, October 5, 1933, p. 14, in which an
airline pilot was ordered reinstated after being discharged without a hearing in
violation of an agreement that a Pilots Council would be consulted in all matters
involving "changes of status." The grievant had been active in union work,
chairman of the Pilots Council, and a representative of the union in dealings
with the employer.

[35] Refer to *Legislative History of the National Labor Relations Act 1935*
(Washington: U. S. Government Printing Office, 1949), Vol. I, pp. 115–130, for
an indignant presentation by William Green of details of the company-union
drive on the part of employers. On p. 117, for example, are copies of three
practically identical letters, each notifying employees of the "inauguration" of a
plan of employee representation. They went out from: Illinois Steel Co. in
Chicago, June 14, 1933; American Steel & Wire Co., Cleveland, June 15, 1933;
and Continental Can Co., Inc., in Harvey, Louisiana, August 7, 1933.

[36] *Decisions 1933–34*, p. 18.

was called by the management. The works manager admitted that he had not only selected those who were to explain the plan to the employees, but that he had also explained it himself in several of the departments of the plant. All of the employees were instructed to vote. Section 7 (a) was not read to them, and they were not afforded an opportunity to pass upon any other form of organization or representation. Nominations were oral. . . . Various officials of the company called off the names of the employees as they proceeded to the ballot box . . . Immediately after the election the length of the terms of the individual representatives were fixed by pulling numbers out of a hat . . . No constitution or by-laws were prepared for the plan either before the election or since, and no collective agreement with the management has ever been reached by the elected representatives. At least two of the elected representatives are assistant foremen.

The Board found that the company had interfered with the rights of its employees and scheduled an election for the free choice of representatives. On the other hand, where the record showed that workers had had an opportunity to choose freely between inside and outside unions, had voted in favor of the former, and had then organized and chosen representatives who bargained with the employer, with no showing of interference or coercion, the Board upheld the choice as coming within the terms of Section 7a.[37]

The Board also went a long way towards formulating the most difficult definition of all—the meaning of "collective bargaining." In the Eagle Rubber Co. case of May 16, 1934 is found language foreshadowing that of the *Taft-Hartley Act* today: [38]

The statute requires the employer to meet with the duly chosen representatives of its employees, whether an employee or outside union, and to negotiate actively in good faith to reach an agreement. Disclosure of those represented is not required. Summary

[37] See Federal Knitting Mills, January 31, 1934, pp. 69–70.
[38] In Sec. 8 (d), Title I, "Amendment of National Labor Relations Act."

rejections of employees' demands and restriction of communication to letters do not constitute compliance with the statute.[39]

and in the Connecticut Coke case, June 20, 1934, the term was fleshed out still further:

> True collective bargaining involves more than the holding of conferences and the exchange of pleasantries. It is not limited to the settlement of specific grievances. Wages, hours, and conditions of employment may properly be the subject of negotiation and collective bargaining. While the law does not compel the parties to reach agreement, it does contemplate that both parties will approach negotiations with an open mind and will make a reasonable effort to reach a common ground of agreement. The definite announcement by the company that it will not make any oral or written agreement deprives collective bargaining of any content or objective.[40]

Such was the tenor of the Board's decisions. In the great majority of cases it was unanimous; the first of very few dissents appeared after the reorganization of March 3, 1934. In the eleven months of its existence, the National Labor Board met and decided almost every major issue subsumed under "the right to organize and bargain collectively free from interference, restraint, or coercion by employers." The positions it took have long since been absorbed into the federal labor code. The work of the (1st) and subsequent National Labor Relations Boards has been essentially a codification and refinement of the original Board's interpretations. The *National Labor Relations Act* itself, a model of clarity and succinctness, as attested by its immunity for twelve years to revision or repeal and its remarkable record before the courts, was a direct outgrowth of the experience under Section 7a.

After an interim of 14 years, the National Labor Board resumed almost precisely at the point where the National War Labor Board of World War I left off. In form of organization,

[39] *Decisions of the National Labor Board April 1934–July 1934*, pp. 31–33.
[40] *Ibid.*, p. 89.

generality of instructions, and manner of functioning, the two were practically identical. Both were *ad hoc,* part-time, tripartite "citizen's" bodies with influential public chairmen. (Ex-President William Howard Taft was chairman of the NWLB.) Both were instructed to mediate disputes between employers and employees (to "consider, adjust, and settle differences and controversies that may arise. . . ."), and both soon found that mediation of the interests of the parties would not suffice; that final and binding third-party rulings were required to establish the new line of demarcation between the rights of employees and the privileges of employers. Under the statutory authority of Sec. 7a, which was but a slightly expanded version of the NWLB's Rule No. 2, the NLB separated out the major issues and ruled on them intelligently and firmly. However, in the stormy days of the early New Deal, its legal base was too frail to stand against the rising current of employer opposition headed by Weirton Steel and the Budd Manufacturing Co.

The difference, in 1933–34, lay in the social and economic revolution that was in the making during the Twenties and the crash which followed. Neither the electorate nor the Federal government was in a mood to settle again (as in 1920) for a short respite from employer autocracy. The NLB became the (1st) NLRB, which in turn became the NLRB of the *Wagner Act,* an administrative commission with instructions, authority and eventually, constitutionality. It took four years, but when it was over, the labor movement promptly doubled in numbers and rose to 15 million by 1946.

It is now well established in the U. S. that employees have the right to organize and bargain collectively. The boundary between Mill's "right to combine" and "harm to others" is still being worked out—by the NLRB, in collective bargaining, in grievance settlements—and in certain cases, controversy is strong (e.g., right-to-work, the Boulwerism issue). Nevertheless, for 20 years union-management negotiation has been the dominant method for settling the terms of employment throughout the basic industries, with repercussions that extend far beyond the boundaries of organized crafts and bargaining units. The labor movement's contribution to national morale and the prosperity of the past two decades may be argued, but that it has been a contribution is no longer at issue.

Varying degrees of recognition have been accorded the people and agencies which had a part in this outcome. However, in reviewing the shifting tides of labor controversy—public and private, in war and in depression, during the past half century—the exceptional service of the two great "citizen's commissions," the National War Labor Board of World War I and the National Labor Board of Section 7a, should receive more than passing mention. Both were called up hurriedly in time of crisis, with little in the way of guidance—and that little, as it turned out, of limited usefulness. Both moved rapidly and surely to the key issue: *how deep to cut into which traditional employer prerogatives.* In doing so, they left for their successors a body of decisions that will bear study today as an authoritative source of principles for disentangling one of the more complex problems of legal relationship in modern society.

Raymond Moley *has been a contributing editor of* News-week *since 1937. He was Professor of Public Law and Government at Columbia University before undertaking to organize the "Brains Trust" for Franklin D. Roosevelt. As Assistant Secretary of State in 1933, he played a central role in the first 100 days of the New Deal. He was editor of* Today *from 1933 to 1937, and has written a score of books, including* After Seven Years, 27 Masters of Politics *and most recently,* The First New Deal.

Rexford G. Tugwell *is now at the Center for the Study of Democratic Institutions in Santa Barbara, California. He was Professor of Economics at Columbia University before coming to the New Deal. As Assistant Secretary of Agriculture in 1933 and Under-Secretary of Agriculture from 1934 through 1937, he played a significant role in shaping the New Deal farm program. He was Governor of Puerto Rico from 1941 through 1946 and after that became Professor of Political Science at the University of Chicago. Among his numerous books are* The Democratic Roosevelt, The Art of Politics, The Enlargement of the Presidency, *and* FDR: Architect of an Era.

Ernest K. Lindley *is Special Assistant to the Secretary of State. He was Washington correspondent of the* New York Herald Tribune *from 1933 through 1937 and chief of the Washington Bureau of* Newsweek *from 1937 through 1961. Among his publications concerning the Thirties are* Franklin D. Roosevelt—a Career in Progressive Democracy, A New Deal for Youth *and* The Roosevelt Revolution.

Symposium: Early Days of the New Deal

Raymond Moley: The limitation of time for these preliminary statements compels certain very dangerous simplifications, perhaps over-simplifications. We are considering a period which, I should suggest, runs from Franklin D. Roosevelt's election in November, 1932, to the summer of 1935 when, I think it is generally recognized, that the first New Deal ended and what has been called the second New Deal began. Most of what is pertinent in that period happened in the year 1933. I shall address myself to that period, which marked the turn of the tide of depression and opened the way to a quite different era—political and economic.

And so we are talking about a far-off time and events of long ago. Over the history of this period there is already growing a sort of mossy mythology. It was another generation, and many of the historians who have written about it were too young to have any personal understanding of what happened at that time. And we, the venerable survivors who are speaking here are members of a very small part of that gay and confident company. A great majority of those who were with us have gone to their last reward—or punishment—whatever is deemed appropriate to the Divine dispenser of justice.

So that we can follow the important events of that time, I suggest dividing the early New Deal into a number of phases. I

[124]

have used these phases to provide the framework of a book over which I have labored more or less intensively for more than nine years.

We three here were very close to the center of things. In the spring of 1932, Roosevelt commissioned me to bring together a group which was subsequently, and I think so far as we were concerned, uncomfortably called the Brains Trust. And the first person that I took to Albany was Rex Tugwell. The second one unfortunately is not here—he could not be here—Adolph Berle. I'd like to say this about Rex—we wouldn't have had a farm program, which I think was the most rational and most successful of all the legislation of the New Deal, if it hadn't been for Rex Tugwell. Ernest Lindley was unquestionably the best informed journalist in Washington about what was going on in the Administration, and to this day, because I have had occasion in the course of working on my own book to consult the vast literature that has accumulated, Ernest Lindley's book, *The Roosevelt Revolution,* which was published late in 1933, is the most authentic history of that period which exists in print. And he knew all about it because he was a friend of ours and we slipped him the information, and he believed that we were doing something, which made it all the better for us.

We were not, I believe, concerned with the purely political activities of that period. We were only collaterally interested in jobs and patronage. We were concerned with ideas and programs.

I recognize six phases in this period. First, after the election in November, 1932, Roosevelt was suddenly confronted with the problem of the debts which Europe owed to us and also international economic relationships, such as the tariff. Very valuable time, which might better have been spent in planning for the new Administration, was spent by Rex Tugwell and me in what might be called a struggle for Roosevelt's mind.

There was a very considerable element in the Democratic Party, largely centered in New York City and in the East, which favored either a cancellation of the debts or a reduction in their amounts. These elements were also favorable to tariff revision and close cooperation with European countries in economic affairs.

Rex and I found that the internationalists in our party were working very closely with members of the outgoing Hoover Administration. Notable among these was Secretary of State Stimson. For a while, in December and January, it was touch and go, although my own political instinct and Tugwell's more comprehensive economic wisdom dictated that we concentrate our attention, at least for the first period of the New Deal, on domestic recovery. We might be called nationalists as distinguished from internationalists. The outcome of that very difficult time was Roosevelt's acceptance of the principle of domestic recovery first. Rex and I won that fight, but only after a pretty bitter struggle.

The second phase was the selection of a Cabinet. To a large extent the Cabinet selections were dictated either by political considerations or personal relationships. I think it is only fair to say, on the basis of my own knowledge, that Tugwell was responsible for the selection of Henry Wallace as Secretary of Agriculture. This assured that the major program of the New Deal, which was advocated in the 1932 campaign, would be the restoration of agriculture, believing, as we did, that if we could get agriculture moving, then the rest of the economy would follow. With two or three exceptions, and I would say Wallace was one of those exceptions, the Roosevelt Cabinet was less distinguished than the average of the previous cabinets. In fact, I think only Wilson's Cabinet rivaled Roosevelt's in mediocrity.

The next phase was forced upon us by the bank crisis, and this occupied all of Roosevelt's attention from before the inauguration until well along in March. I was in the middle of this, since I was very close to Will Woodin, the New Secretary of the Treasury, and I can speak with some authority about what was done. What really happened was that all of the measures that were taken to rescue the banks were already considered and thought out in the Hoover Administration, particularly in the Treasury. Hoover, however, because he could not decide upon such a drastic measure as closing the banks by Presidential proclamation, failed to use these tools.

Roosevelt, in effect, took over these ideas and, in fact, the Hoover team—consisting mostly of Arthur Ballantine, Under Secretary of the Treasury, and Gloyd Awalt, Acting Comptroller of the Currency, and others. It was a very successful operation and, in my judgment, projected the new Administration into a climate of confidence which marked the beginning of recovery. At that moment there was no politics involved because we were all trying to save the system in order to stimulate the confidence that was necessary to the recovery of the whole economy.

The next phase consisted of a budget of legislation which was passed by Congress during the famous Hundred Days' session. As I reflect upon these measures, it seems to me that the major gain that was made was that there was so much legislation in so short a time that the public, without knowing much about any of these measures, was inspirited to believe that something was happening, and that that provided the stimulus to confidence which carried us through into the first phase of recovery. In other words, if you give people the idea that something good for them is happening, it doesn't matter much what it is; they'll start working, and they'll start spending, and things will start rolling. It was the restoration of confidence under the infinitely inspiriting leadership of Roosevelt himself, because he looked confident, he spoke of confidence, and he made everybody believe in themselves.

Phase five was essentially a revival of certain international complications which, as Ernest Lindley called it in his book, was the New Deal in the Old World, and I got caught there in a crossfire of misunderstandings. Most of this centered in the calling of the Economic Conference in London in June. My own conclusion about that, since I was so deeply involved, is that it was unfortunate that the Conference could not have been continued. At any rate, we should have informed Europe that the United States would, within the limitations imposed upon us by our domestic necessities, contribute to world stabilization.

The next phase was, so far as possible, a series of measures which would provide relief for the vast number of unemployed and distressed people. This was a very serious problem that went on into the fall and winter of 1933 and 1934.

I offer my over-all judgment that Roosevelt's capacity to project his own confidence in the future, his willingness to try hitherto untried measures, the evangelical efforts of members of the New Deal, such as Hugh Johnson, and also the cooperation of Congress, made possible the success of what is usually attributed to the First New Deal.

I have emphasized in the foregoing the element of public confidence, and that isn't just business confidence, but public confidence generally. I shall avoid, until we have a general discussion here, any consideration of the specific measures, their value, and their results.

Rexford Tugwell: I thought I might go a little further back than Ray has done and speak of the year 1932 instead of 1933, because I think that that was the time when most of these things that happened in 1933 were really shaped. That was the time that Ray had the job of sitting across the table finally with Mr. Roosevelt, with the draft of a speech and reading it to him and having Mr. Roosevelt say what he wanted crossed out and what he wanted put in and making those flourishes which made it his own rather than someone else's. But this was Ray's responsibility. The rest of us were never present when this final operation took place. But this didn't mean that we didn't do a lot of preliminary work and a lot of verifying and a lot of gathering of information and even a lot of discussing, because we met many times in that early spring in Albany for quite general discussions of memoranda that some of us may have doctored up. And Ray joined with us in those discussions. You must remember that, although he had been in the federal government some years before, Roosevelt had been an Assistant Secretary of the Navy, essentially an administrator, and he hadn't dealt essentially with national problems in any general way. And since that time he had been Governor of New York. But in none of these positions had he been up against national problems, having to think about them in any really concerted way and, when it seemed likely that he was going to be President or that he hoped to be President at least, it was necessary to think about them and have some kind of plan about them. This was particularly true because the country was in the midst of a depression. It's very difficult to realize what Roosevelt was going to be up against and what he knew he was going to be up against if he did become President. And so an explanation of the Depression and some idea of how recovery could be brought about was very important to him.

Not too much in a specific way was said about this during the campaign. He did make a promise to relieve unemployment, but he also promised to do some other things which weren't entirely consistent with it, such as balancing the budget and making economies enough to pay for all the unemployment relief he was going to provide. Ray has pointed out in some of his writings, particularly in *After Seven Years,* how inconsistent some of these were. But, at the time, I suppose the excuse was that they were good politics. And I give Ray credit for having always warned Roosevelt when he was being inconsistent. Of course he couldn't force the President to be consistent, but he could tell him when he was being inconsistent. He said there was a struggle for Roosevelt's mind during the early days of the New Deal. I say there was a struggle for Roosevelt's mind even during this period, because I think that the three of us here represented a more advanced or a different kind of progressivism than was popular at that time. I think you could have called us, perhaps, collectivists or something of that sort. At any rate, we didn't believe that recovery was to be brought about by punishing people in Wall Street; we thought that you had to do something more profound than that. Roosevelt was always going off and wanting to tear the speculators limb from limb. That was all right with us, but we didn't think it was going to get anything going again, and we thought it necessary to have some plan for recovery. At any rate, we did discuss these matters with him, and I don't think we won this really.

He did have one put over on him which neither Ray nor I had anything to do with. Ernest K. Lindley wrote the Oglethorpe Speech. Roosevelt was out of our control at that time, being in Warm Springs, but he was exposed to these radical influences represented by Lindley, and he came out with a speech in which he said that what this country needs is bold experimentation and planning. Well, I asked Ernest if he recalled how quick the reaction to that came from Louis Howe and the politicians, and he said he didn't really remember that; but I remember it very well. They said this is stuff that we don't want you to deal with any more, this is not good for the farmers to hear, or for the people out West to hear, and these grand general ideas about planning and about experimentation are not good politics. So we never heard any more about that and I think we were all sorry, for we would like to have seen Roosevelt develop what he meant by planning more. This I think we lost out on, and you may be surprised to hear me say that we lost out to a person who was never visible. That was Justice Brandeis, the prophet of the old kind of progressivism which believed in the anti-trust laws and breaking everything up and having small units competing with each other so that there was nothing for the government to do except to carry out this breaking-up process. But he was stronger than we were, and the reason he was stronger was that the politicians agreed with him.

Of course, there was another competing influence all through this early period and it came from business sources, really. Businessmen, a great many of them, were sympathetic to the idea of planning and were writing about planning in those days. But they were consumed with the notion that if Roosevelt simply made no promises of any considerable sort and didn't threaten anybody, that businessmen would have their confidence restored, and they would put their factories to work and unemployment would be ended in that way. I think they had a considerable influence on Roosevelt. At least he stopped all this talk about planning and collectivization, and when the election came, he really was a man without a mandate. He had said a number of things which led people to believe that they might hope that he would do something about unemployment and that he would get activities started again. But nobody, I think, had any definite idea of what the scheme would be that he would follow out. So when the New Deal measures came, in what's called the First Hundred Days, I think that they came, for most people, simply out of the blue. I don't think that they expected them in any definite way.

Ernest K. Lindley: I must emphasize that I wasn't a member of the Brains Trust although, as Mr. Tugwell indicated, I had a hand in an important speech, maybe another one or two later on. I'm somewhat junior. I was not a college professor, so I wasn't qualified to be in the Brains Trust. I was just a journalist. But I am a senior here in one respect: my connection with Roosevelt began before either Mr. Moley's or Mr. Tugwell's. And as a matter of fact, in 1931 I wrote the first biography of Franklin Roosevelt, called *Franklin D. Roosevelt, A Career in Progressive Democracy*.

I must begin a dissent here. Despite the very great contributions which the Brains Trust made, it is true that Mr. Roosevelt had a few ideas before the Brains Trust came into being. As a Roosevelt, he had married another Roosevelt, the niece of President T. R. Roosevelt, and he had naturally followed the career of T. R. very closely. He went into the Wilson Administration as Assistant Secretary of the Navy. He had advocated the nomination of Wilson, and he was very much devoted to the New Freedom. Then he was nominated for Vice-President and went all over the country preaching the liberal doctrine as well as support of the League of Nations. And, during the ensuing seven or eight years, while he was suffering from polio and its after effects, he paid great attention to national affairs.

I don't want to belittle in the slightest the immense contribution made by my friends, but neither of them was even mentioned in the book I wrote about Roosevelt in 1931. They came on to the scene the following year. Mr. Moley had been working on a crime commission report for the state of New York, but I didn't happen to deal with that in my book and I don't think I had even seen the report. Mr. Roosevelt was very much committed in his thinking as Governor—before the Brains Trust came into being—to some of the central ideas that have come down through the Square Deal of Theodore Roosevelt and the New Freedom of Woodrow Wilson. He was particularly well developed in his thinking about conservation. In fact, he revived that as a great movement in the United States, the first movement having occurred under Theodore Roosevelt with Pinchot and others. He also had some rather advanced ideas on such questions as abolishing the poor house and substituting aid for the elderly, ideas in the social insurance field, and in the whole field of labor legislation—which came naturally from his association with the northern wing of the Democratic party in New York, that had begun to move in that direction about 1910 and 1911. That was when Franklin D. Roosevelt made his debut as a state legislator and came in contact with Al Smith, Robert F. Wagner, and others who went on to great things in the Democratic Party.

I could enumerate other things that he stood for already, including the shorter work week, cheap electricity, and a number of others. But I think the important distinction was that he did not, when he first began to think about the Presidency, anticipate that he would run in a year of a great depression. His thinking was more along the lines of the traditional reforms, resuming them, carrying them forward—things that would have been done and needed to be done quite irrespective of the economic conditions of the country. It was the continuing depression, which became worse in 1931 and in early 1932, which made it necessary for him to gather together a group of people who could give him some advice on how to deal with the problems of that great economic disaster. And I think that is the reason the Brains Trust came into existence, although its contributions in the ensuing period were not purely limited to measures of recovery. I think some of the important longer range reforms originated with the Brains Trust also. But I would draw that important distinction.

I do want to mention, before I relinquish this platform momentarily, a rather interesting event which I think historically assumes a great deal of significance in my mind. That was a day in May, I believe it was 1932, when a few of us [—I think there were four journalists—] were down at Warm Springs with Franklin D. Roosevelt. That was about the time of the Oglethorpe Speech. And, incidentally, the way that speech came to be written was that Sam Rosenman brought down his speech. I don't know whether he had written it or the Brains Trust had written it, but Roosevelt showed it to three or four of us and we said it was too tepid; it didn't say anything. He said, "Well if you can do better, you write one." So we undertook to do it. It ended with my writing it. I started about four o'clock in the afternoon and ended about four o'clock the next morning, and I was astonished when FDR used it practically word for word as I wrote it. He put a couple of paragraphs in at the beginning. The only political reaction I got to that speech at the time was from Dick Russell, who was then Governor of Georgia and who was on the platform and introduced FDR. He said to me afterwards: "That was a courageous speech." But the speech, I think, contained Roosevelt's pragmatic approach, combined with his willingness to experiment. I knew him well enough; I wasn't trying to thrust something down his throat—I knew his general approach.

In his approach to the Depression particularly, he had no one economic theory. In fact, he distrusted all economic theories. His approach was "try something and, if that doesn't work, try something else." And, incidentally, Arthur Schlesinger, Jr. was incorrect in his book when he says that I was under the influence of Rex Tugwell and Adolph Berle when I wrote that speech; I had not had the pleasure of meeting either one of them at the time. Adolph Berle's book, *The Modern Corporation and Private Property* (with Means), had not even been published yet. I may have read an article or two by Rex Tugwell, but Schlesinger was wrong in that respect, as I have found him wrong in other respects as a historian.

But the event I wanted to mention was the day that a very attractive and dynamic and wealthy man from Boston whose name was Joseph Patrick Kennedy came down to Warm Springs. Wealthy people were very scarce in the Roosevelt camp at that time. We were having a picnic, incidentally, out on a mountaintop with four journalists and Missy LeHand and the Governor's bodyguard and FDR. Along came Joe Kennedy in his city clothes, accompanied by his friend and guide, Edward Moore, a former Boston newspaper man (for whom Teddy Kennedy—Edward Moore Kennedy—was named). Out they came, and they had not seen Franklin Roosevelt since the First World War when young Joe Kennedy was managing one of the Bethlehem steel ship plants in Massachusetts. He had not declared for FDR then, and we had a rather free-for-all discussion at the picnic. What was this multi-millionaire doing down there with a socialist like Franklin D. Roosevelt? The newspapermen were needling him. Joe Kennedy knew he was being needled, but I think he thought maybe there was a little bit underneath. Finally he said, "Why I'd give half of what I got to get this country on its feet again." And one of us said: "Joe, that's not enough." When he left, he declared for FDR. And, as a result of that, of course, he came into the New Deal as an administrator and then as an Ambassador. I wonder very much whether John F. Kennedy would have ever got into politics if that meeting hadn't occurred at that time. So I look back on that as a very interesting link between the Roosevelt Administration and the Kennedy Administration.

I would emphasize that many of the things we take for granted today originated in that period: our social insurance system; the use of taxation and various other kinds of fiscal management to keep the economy going; the acceptance by the government of the general responsibility for a suitable economic environment; collective bargaining; and the five-day week. I remember very well when Heywood Broun and myself went to FDR. This was in the days of the NRA. Hugh Johnson, being good at public relations, didn't want to offend the newspapers by imposing the five-day week on them; but we thought he should, and FDR called Hugh Johnson over there and told him to apply it to the newspapers. It finally ended in compromise: a 5-day week only on the papers in the larger cities—and they screamed. I expected to be fired from the *Herald Tribune* at any moment. But that's where the five-day week began—in that period.

I could mention many other things—the purification of the securities market, banking reforms, deposit insurance, and a whole range of reforms. Incidentally, just as I was leaving Washington this morning, I ran into several people who were assembling to celebrate the twentieth anniversary of the *Full Employment Act* of 1946, which is an outgrowth of the New Deal and which formalizes, perhaps inadequately, the acceptance by the federal government of the responsibility for taking measures to promote full employment and keep the economy going at full face.

Raymond Moley: To Mr. Lindley's point that Roosevelt had all these ideas prior to the appearance of we saviors, let me say that the major piece of legislation was the enactment of the farm program. This was called the Domestic Allotment Plan and Rex here was the only one of our group who understood this and sold Roosevelt on it. There was another plan called the McNary-Haugen Plan. It had been passed three times and vetoed during the Republican years, and was entirely different in many ways from the Domestic Allotment Plan. When Roosevelt announced in his acceptance speech in Chicago that he was going to support the Domestic Allotment Plan, Henry Morgenthau went to him and said, "But in February you came out for the McNary-Haugen Bill." And Roosevelt said, "Oh that was February." So, at any rate, if he had all these ideas before, we sorted them out and got the ones into his mind that would be consistently campaign material.

Of course, there's always the question of who provided the words and who provided the tune. I'm reminded of a story about Mark Twain. Mark Twain was said to be a very profane individual and his wife decided that she would break him of the habit. Mark was sitting in his bed writing and his wife came in and exploded a series of barnyard oaths to him, and Mark looked up at her and said, "Darling you've got the words, but you haven't got the tune." So there was a great deal of sorting out of ideas, and I think that Rex and I would agree that we probably never did get them sorted out, but we got a lot of them over. All of these things are a matter of compromise, of collective thinking, and so on.

Toward the end of September, in 1932, we felt that the election was in the bag and, at that time, I asked Adolph Berle to put together in a memorandum the various positions that Roosevelt had taken in the campaign which would be useful in a program for him after he had been inaugurated. And he did so. To a large degree that memorandum, which was sent to me on November 10, 1932, is a fairly good list of the measures that were passed by Congress in the Hundred Days. There were different authors, and there were measures that represented different economic views. We were trying to apply remedies according to the dictates of common sense. I don't think we had much use for a philosophy in those days. The point is that the philosophies of what happened in those days come from people who didn't know anything about what happened then. As my old teacher, Professor Dunning, once said in his presidential address before the American Historical Association, by the time a system of philosophy has been created, the world upon which it is based has passed away. And if we, the Brains Trust, had tried to create a system of philosophy, the country would have gone to hell. We were just doing things that needed to be done. And let the fellows who are writing now, who weren't alive then, write up the philosophy. That's all right—like Schlesinger, for example. Some of the things in his book are enshrined now as fictional masterpieces.

Rexford Tugwell: I had some influence with him about one of those fictional masterpieces because, like most of the Harvard people, he insisted that John Maynard Keynes had invented the New Deal. He sent me this passage before his book was published and I did succeed in getting him to modify it a little bit by explaining to him that Keynes hadn't shown up in this country until 1934. It just happens that Keynes, when he came over here in 1934, came to me because he had an introduction from somebody over there. I was the one who introduced him to Roosevelt, and I'll never forget what Roosevelt said afterwards. "Well," he said, "that damned Englishman is trying to tell us what we're doing already."

Raymond Moley: I saw him in the summer of 1933 when I attended the London Economic Conference which ended disastrously, not the meeting with Keynes. After Roosevelt pulled the rug out from under Mr. Hull—and everybody there who represented the United States and everybody over here who was trying to advise him—Keynes came out with a statement in a newspaper abroad saying that Roosevelt was magnificent. But on this matter of Keynes' contribution to the New Deal, the idea of spending money for recovery is commonplace; Rex was for it before we ever heard of Keynes.

Ernest K. Lindley: I would like to emphasize that this is what I regard as a very important distinction here between the recovery programs, including agriculture—because we had had severe agricultural problems for quite a while—and some of the others. Now TVA, which was one of the great accomplishments of the New Deal, practically was unfolded by FDR. I don't think that anyone in the Brains Trust had very much to do with that, and FDR carried it far beyond what George Norris had done.

Raymond Moley: I never heard of it and I never agreed with it.

Ernest K. Lindley: Well, there you are. Yet this concept of the coordinated development of an entire river valley came out of the old progressive movement, plus various other sources. I remember when FDR unfolded that at his press conference in Warm Springs. It ran about an hour and a half, if I remember correctly, and it went far beyond anything I had ever heard before from any other person in that field. FDR had thought a great deal about these problems that were not particularly related to the Depression. It was the Depression that really brought you people into the picture, and that's where I think the Brains Trust, as I said, made an important contribution to longer range reform. Your big job was to find some way to get us out of a depression which had this country, I think, almost at the point of a breakup.

Raymond Moley: Well, all right, we'll take credit for everything, except that we didn't create the Depression.

Rexford Tugwell: As a matter of fact, Ray, you couldn't really say that we cured it, either. We didn't get unemployment down under eight million all the time I was in Washington at least.

Raymond Moley: Rex, I think we would both agree that the New Deal ended in 1935, and that Roosevelt scrapped all ideological things then. I think he got tired of ideological matters and he scrapped the idea of planning after the Supreme Court had declared the NRA unconstitutional, and also when the Court declared the AAA unconstitutional. I have always believed that the farm program was a constructive thing and that the program, along with the general restoration of confidence, would have gotten us out of the Depression. I think that the Supreme Court was wrong when they declared it unconstitutional, and I think that Rex Tugwell was more responsible for this farm program than anybody else.

Rexford Tugwell: We made one mistake only and, of course, that was the grounds on which it was declared unconstitutional—hitching the tax to it. If we hadn't had the processing tax in it, I think it wouldn't have been invalidated. I will say this, that the bill which was passed in its place, which was called the Conservation Act, was a much better bill than our original one.

Raymond Moley: That's what Wallace thought.

Ernest K. Lindley: May I make an observation here? I don't think the New Deal came to an end in 1935. I think that's when the Brains Trust's influence began to diminish. Ray Moley remained a very powerful factor in the New Deal several years after he left the State Department. He came down regularly to work on various speeches and programs for FDR. And, of course, Rex Tugwell continued in the government. After the 1936 election, we had the maximum-hour and minimum-wage legislation and a number of new laws in the conservation field.

Then there was legislation carrying forward slum clearance and beginning the attack on some of the problems of our cities. It was not really until 1938 that Roosevelt began to put domestic things aside. That was the time of Munich, and then the war began to loom in Europe—that's when he did a great half-turn in order to bring the conservatives in the Party back in support of things he felt had to be done on the international scene. I would say, starting early in 1939 or late in 1938, the international scene definitely was dominant. And it was not only the Brains Trust, but it was some of the second New Dealers of the Brandeis school, who began to weep at that time because their reforms were being sidetracked before they had been put into effect.

Raymond Moley: That was a good thing. But let me explain this. In the years from 1933 to 1936, the gross national product increased ten per cent a year. Between 1933 and 1936 unemployment went down 2.8 million. From 1936 to 1940, the gross national product increased only two and a half per cent a year. In other words, in four years it increased only as much as it increased in one year when we were around. And unemployment went up until 1940 by 800,000. So you see, things didn't go very well after we left.

Moderator: What was the major change after the first New Deal in 1935?

Raymond Moley: The major change was pure political opportunism. Roosevelt's speeches then sounded—Rex said so in his book, didn't you?—like William Jennings Bryan.

Rexford Tugwell: If I didn't say it, I will in my next book.

Raymond Moley: You said it in your book, you've got it there, and I've quoted you in my book. So I think there was a definite break—even Schlesinger knows that.

Rexford Tugwell: I think I would agree with Ray, but I would bring in another factor which it won't do to overlook. And that is, immediately after his great victory in 1936, Roosevelt took on the Supreme Court. He hadn't had an opportunity to appoint any judges up to then, and they had turned down two or three of the important New Deal acts—declared them unconstitutional. This so annoyed him, and he felt he had so much strength because of his electoral victory, that he could take on the Supreme Court. Well, he got a tremendous reaction to it and this consolidated the liaison between the Southern conservatives and the Republicans to the extent that he was never able to get anything else done of any importance, although I don't know but what he felt the New Deal was fairly finished by that time.

Ernest K. Lindley: He told me after the 1936 election that he felt the country could stand commotion and change for only so long and he intended not to ask for much new legislation in his second term. It's quite true that he had to give battle to the Court because it stood as a barrier to carrying out some very important things, and, while he was defeated in his efforts to enlarge the Court, he won the war because the Court began to change sides. Owen Roberts and Charles Evans Hughes changed over, and they began to approve things in principle that they had rejected before. In fact, there were some direct reversals of decisions.

Rexford Tugwell: The point I wanted to make was not about the Court, but rather, that the "court-packing" plan so encouraged the Democratic reactionaries and conservatives, whatever you want to call them, that they did keep this liaison with the Republicans from then on until the war came.

Ernest K. Lindley: Yes, but that was a very short period. Nevertheless, we got in that period the minimum-wage and maximum-hour legislation, and some conservation measures. You got the WPA, or the equivalent of it, carried forward. I think the reason that you weren't more successful on the economic side—you see I'm dissociating myself from this—was that you were too timid in injecting what had to be injected into the economy. You were applying measures in part which would have worked well in 1930 but, by the time 1933 came along, we were so far down that our industrial depression was exceeded in the world, or equalled, only by that in Germany. Our agricultural depression was as deep as any in the world—and most of the agricultural countries had taken somewhat effective measures to bring up the prices of raw commodities before we began moving here.

Rexford Tugwell: I don't know why you look at me and say you. I mean, you were there, too.

Ernest K. Lindley: Well, I was just an observer. You were just too timid. I tried to sell you as a conservative, Rex. I told everybody that you were really a conservative, but they wouldn't believe me.

Rexford Tugwell: I never did feel that the measures taken were massive enough. I think you know that I didn't feel that.

Raymond Moley: In general, I think that the 1933 period was a period of rather orthodox and conservative reforms that were essential: the permanent banking reforms and the agricultural reforms. Agriculture did start to recover with the help of the drought in 1934.

Ernest K. Lindley: I do think that one would have to say, looking back—at least I would say—that what was done then saved the free enterprise system in this country. What was done, was called, at that time, socialistic, communistic, fascist. But it saved that free enterprise system and gave it more humanitarian, more effective aspects, and led to other reforms which followed the war and developed further into the economic management by the central government which we have today.

Rexford Tugwell: Did Roosevelt ever explain to you in those days why he never attempted to revive the NRA as he did the AAA?

Ernest K. Lindley: I think he decided that the code system was not a good thing in every respect, and that he should take certain elements out of the NRA—such as collective bargaining, the maximum work week and the minimum wage—and enact them separately. I think he was very much disturbed by some of the business codes when he took another look at them.

Rexford Tugwell: But I have always felt that the principle of NRA ought to have been carried on, and he ought to have done it.

Raymond Moley: The trouble was that he tried to do too much under the NRA. One of the humorists said that the trouble with Napoleon was that he tried to do too much and he done it; and that's what ended the NRA.

Upton Sinclair *is a prominent American writer of social protest whose novels include* The Journal of Arthur Stirling *(1903),* Manassas *(1904),* The Jungle *(1906), a study of social conditions in the Chicago stockyards,* Love's Pilgrimage *(1911),* King Coal *(1917) and* Oil *(1927). He organized the EPIC movement in California and captured the Democratic nomination for governor of that state in 1934. Although defeated at the polls, his campaign drew wide national attention.*

How I Reformed Three
Great American Families

THE THREE FAMILIES that I reformed were the Armours, the Rockefellers, and the Fords. I amuse myself by saying that I reformed them, but at the same time, I'll show you that I'm not just being funny.

In 1904, we had a little Socialist paper in the United States, a four-page weekly called *The Appeal to Reason*. It had about half a million circulation, and in that paper I read accounts of the horrors that were being perpetrated against the striking workers in the stockyards of Chicago. I told the editor that I thought it might be a good idea for me to go there and write up what was happening. So I went to Chicago and put myself in the charge of the workers and they took me in and told me to put on old clothes. Then they took me around and told me what to do. I got a dinner pail, and, if you've got old clothes on and carry a dinner pail, you can go anywhere in the stockyards—even in the most secret rooms where they're perpetrating any horrible thing. They assume you're on the way to the next room job, and nobody pays any attention to you. I wandered around the stockyards that way for several weeks. I would spend the evenings in the homes of the workers, and they'd get half a dozen of them together. There was a doctor who was sympathetic and a lawyer who was sympathetic and a businessman and so on, and I learned everything about those stockyards.

I had the advantage of advice from a specialist in stockyards, an Englishman, who was a regular staff writer for the leading medical paper in England. What he didn't know about the stockyards no one knew. This Englishman said to me, "Mr. Sinclair, these are not slaughterhouses; these are something for which there is no name. The horrors they are perpetrating here are beyond belief." And then, of course, I knew I had an expert and I wasn't making a fool of myself. So I went home and started to write this novel about life in the stockyards. I wrote the story and published it serially in *The Appeal to Reason,* and when I began getting letters, I knew I had something that people were interested in. At the last minute a publisher came along and took a chance on publishing it as a book and nobody sued him. So *The Jungle* came out and went all over the world, and it's been translated into ninety languages. Of course, it suited the business people in other countries to read terrible things about America, and maybe that had something to do with the success of the book. But the point is that the facts were there and the reforms began.

I had a very curious experience after the book had been out for a few months. I was camping out in the Adirondacks, and happened to meet a family that was also camping there. I discovered that the young lady in the family was the daughter of the head of Ogden Armour's legal department. She told me how her father and his lawyers had labored for a week or two, day and night, to sway Mr. Armour from his determination to have me arrested for criminal libel. They knew what I had, and what I could have produced in court, and they labored with him and beat him down. Mr. Armour gave way. The practices in question were abandoned, the stockyards were cleaned up, and the workers today have strong unions. Of course, Mr. Armour had to do something to set his name straight before the world, so he built that wonderful Armour Institute in Chicago, where they train people in all kinds of techniques that I don't even know the names of. And there have been no more strikes in the stockyards, the workers have their unions, they get living wages, and the place is as clean as I presume the stockyards can be.

I'd like to end my tale about the stockyards by telling how, a year later, when spending the winter in Bermuda writing another book, I was walking along a country road and came to a little grocery store. I went in to buy something to eat and happened to lift my eyes up. There on the top shelf, completely covered with dust, was a stack of flat cans, which I recognized as Armour's Roast Beef. I said to the proprietor, "What's that up there?" And he said, "Oh, a fella wrote a book about that stuff, and I've never been about to sell a can of it since." Well, anyway, that was the Armours.

Next, the situation with the Rockefellers. I guess they're the wealthiest family in America. They have palaces in the suburbs above New York and they are, of course, one of the most famous names in America. Out in the Rockies, they owned and controlled an iron mine called the Colorado Fuel and Iron Company. They had work camps up there which they ran exactly like slave pens. The workers came in and stayed there and couldn't come out until their time was up. Nobody could get into the camps for they were guarded just like fortresses, and conditions were very hard.

Well, those conditions didn't go over so well with the workers, and they went out on strike. The Western Federation of Miners was in charge, and of course that's a big union, and they had money and built a tent colony down in a little valley-town called Ludlow. There the strikers held out all winter. Of course, this was all very inconvenient to the Rockefeller family, for they were losing a lot of money and I guess they had contracts to supply iron ore that they didn't have. When the strike became intolerable to them, after three or four months, they sent out their gunmen. I say "they," but I don't know who gave the orders. It may have been the superintendent at the mine. I can't say it was the Rockefeller family that did it, but they knew what was being done, certainly. Their gunmen came down in the night and they poured gasoline on the strikers' tents and set fire to them. Well, I suppose they thought it would be easy to get out of a tent. But when the tent is tied up for the winter and you're inside, it's not easy to get out quick, and I think it was three women and eleven children that were burned to death. It is known as "The Ludlow Massacre."

I read about the incident in the *New York Times,* and the wife of the mine union president came to New York and told the story at a meeting in Carnegie Hall. When I heard her, I blew up and invited her to go down with me and tell her story to Mr. Rockefeller. So we sent a little note asking him to meet with us, and his secretary came out and said "No." So then I wrote him a second note and said that if he didn't consent to talk to us, I was going to brand him for murder before the American people. And the answer to that was, "No." So we got a group of folks together and planned what we were going to call The Mourning Parade. We would put a band of mourning crepe around our left arm and walk up and down in front of Mr. Rockefeller's office without speaking a word to anyone, no matter what was done. We started out. Early in the morning I found three ladies ready to start working, so we four walked up and down.

Of course, we'd given warning to the newspapers about what we were going to do, and the police were there and told us to go and walk somewhere else, and we politely said, "No." We were arrested. An officer grabbed me by the arm and started to hustle me along, and I said to the officer, "Please behave like a gentleman. I have no idea but to go with you." After that, he was polite. I thereupon told him the whole story of the Ludlow Massacre and, when we got to the stationhouse—myself and the three ladies—I told the story to the sergeant at the desk. I don't know how much he wrote down, but I was taken across the street to the Court House, and there's a second story bridge that goes across called the Bridge of Sighs. So they took us across the Bridge of Sighs and then we were in a little court room and the officer testified that my conduct was that of a perfect gentleman. That was the only testimony given, where-upon the judge found me guilty of disorderly conduct and fined me $3.00. I refused to pay the fine, of course, and the ladies with me also refused. We were then all taken to jail and the story made all the newspapers.

The newspapers carried a great deal about the Ludlow Mas-sacre and about our Broadway Demonstration, as we called it, and we kept that demonstration going for about three weeks. I paid a $1.00 fine, stayed in jail for two days and had the very interesting experience of being confined with a young thief who told me all about his profession. It's useful, of course, for a writer to know about thieves as well as other people. But I finally paid the dollar because, otherwise, I couldn't appeal the case. So we came out and kept the demonstration going and some young anarchists came along and asked us if they could walk with us and we told them they could walk like anybody else. All they had to do was to keep their promise that they wouldn't speak one word and wouldn't offer resistance to any-thing that was done. So long as they walked with us it was all right, but they made the mistake of going to Tarrytown and there they were stoned and beaten and driven down to the depot by a mob. I don't know whether the Rockefellers put the town ruffians up to it or just how it happened. Well, a group of them—three or four—went into a little room in a tenement in Harlem and proceeded to make a dynamite bomb, but they weren't very expert at making it and blew themselves up. The bomb went off and blew out the whole front of the building and how it happened God only knows, but one of those fellows slid down in the debris and got away.

The point about all that was the effect it had on the Rockefeller family. We hadn't set the anarchists on them, but there the anarchists were. I can imagine those Rockefeller ladies imagining the anarchists with their bombs hiding in the bushes or behind trees and bombing them when they came in at night. It was a doggone uncomfortable thought. So what happened? The Rockefeller family gave up—they reformed. John D. Rockefeller went out to his mines and sat down with the leaders of the mine workers. They worked out the terms to open up those camps and make them civilized places where civilized men could do honest work and get paid and be free to come out and live the lives of American citizens. And that's the way I reformed the Rockefeller family.

I don't know if anybody now has ever heard of old Mother Jones, but she was a wild-eyed old Irish woman who was red-hot blazing for the cause of labor. Wherever there was a strike, Mother Jones would show up and make wild speeches in which she called for the massacre of the masters. She threatened them all with the wrath of heaven and hell and called them all the names that she could think of. She was well known all over America as a great character—by that I mean her stories were always funny. When that agreement had been worked out up in those Rocky Mountain camps, they had a dinner dance and John D. Rockefeller, Jr. danced with old Mother Jones. From that time on, there were no more strikes on any Rockefeller property. And the family, in an effort to take away the horror of the Ludlow Massacre from their family history, set up the

Rockefeller Institute and spent millions of dollars doing all kinds of useful things in America—making great scientific and medical discoveries. If you read scientific papers and magazines, there's not a day that you won't read of some kind of important research being carried on at the Rockefeller Institute.

The most comical thing of all was that poor old John D., the great grandfather of the family, got some kind of counselor or publicity man. And the best thing that publicity man could think up was for old John D. to get a sackful of dimes and go out into the street and give them away to children. I can't think of anything in this world more pathetic than the confession of sin and the apology and atonement of the Rockefeller family.

Now the third family to be reformed was the family of Henry Ford. I never met either of the other two gentlemen that I've been telling about, but I happened to know Henry Ford quite well. He spent a winter in Pasadena and I wrote him a note offering to call on him and was invited to come. He rented almost a palace—a very fine home—with a steel fence all around it somewhere in Pasadena. In the room where we talked there was also Henry's wife. She was a quiet little gentlewoman and played a very important part in this story, although I only saw her this once. I had a somewhat casual impression of her; she was quiet as a little mouse. She was introduced and she greeted me as a hostess does and then she went and sat on a stiff chair against the wall. I can't recall that she spoke one word until, of course, I was ready to go and then she thanked me for coming and bade me good-bye. But it was all so casual and everyday-obvious that it made very little impression on me. I sat and talked with Henry for a couple of hours.

Of course, when I talk to anybody important like Henry I have only one thought in mind, and that is to make a socialist out of him. So I told him what I thought were the responsibilities of the great masters of industry and how industry must ultimately be democratized. It has been my life thesis that autocracy in industry is absolutely incompatible with democracy in politics, and that the two struggle with each other and one or the other will win. I wanted democracy to win, of course. I wanted Ford to introduce democracy gradually into his great institution. Let the workers have their representatives and let them speak for their needs and wishes. Let them sit down with the board of directors and let it be democratic government in industry instead of a monarchy or empire. But, with Henry, it was an empire and he was the emperor. He had no use whatever for the ideas I had suggested to him, but he was perfectly polite and friendly. I guess he'd never heard such queer ideas before.

What I remember most vividly was that little quiet woman who sat in a chair against the wall. What was going on in her mind while I was talking industrial democracy to her husband? Well, anyhow Henry and I liked each other and we got along very nicely and he invited me for a walk in the hills. He liked to walk in the hills. So we walked and all the time I argued industrial democracy with him. We'd sit down on a rock when we got tired, and I explained to him the idea of democracy applied to industry. And he would explain to me how important it was that industry should have a man at the head who really understood everything and had the final say. In other words, he wanted an industrial empire and he had it and I told him so. I said, "Mr. Ford, why don't you start a magazine, and discuss these questions and let both sides be heard? You are finding this discussion interesting and I'm finding you interesting, and why don't you have a magazine and discuss it so that your workers can understand it and form their own ideas?" And he said, "I think that's a good idea. I believe I'll do it." So he went back to Dearborn, Michigan and bought a magazine called the *Dearborn Independence* and made it the very worst magazine ever published in America, without exception. It had no ideas of any liberal or intelligent character. It was just propaganda and cheap stuff to keep the workers ignorant and degraded as they were supposed to be.

Well, the time came when the workers went out on strike.
They wouldn't tolerate Henry's ideas any longer. They formed
their great union and went on strike and they were treated with
brutality beyond belief. Victor Reuther, Walter's brother, was
almost killed. I was living in Pasadena at the time and used
to go over to Hollywood occasionally and was invited to a
dinner party there with movie people. The guest of honor at
that party was Frank Murphy, the newly-elected mayor of Detroit. He was a liberal and I heard him say at the party, "Henry
Ford employs some of the worst gangsters in Detroit and I can
name them." That's how far I had got in my efforts to reform
Henry Ford. But it didn't depend on me, fortunately. Those
men were organized, thirty or forty thousand of them, and they
got real leaders—the two Reuther brothers. Those men knew
what was what, and they put Henry through the grill. Victor
was almost killed, but he survived. I've had the pleasure of
knowing both of them since then.

I was so outraged by the whole thing that I wrote a novelette
of nearly 30,000 words called *The Flivver King*, which was
Henry's life story. Of course, having met him, I could tell all
about him. I mean, I knew him as a personality and could draw
a picture of him and make him talk the way he actually talked.
I wrote this novel and sent proofs of it to the Reuthers. I told
them they could have 200,000 copies in pamphlet form at what
I paid the printer to distribute to Ford workers all over the
world, and they agreed. In my photographs and papers at the
Lilly Library of the University of Indiana, there is a photograph
of the van in which the copies reached the office of the United
Automobile Workers. So every Ford worker in the world—not
merely in the United States, but through all the Ford plants all
over the world—got a copy of that little pamphlet. It's a little
too big to go into your back pocket, but if you fold it once the
wrong way, it slips in very nicely. I was told that in every Ford
plant all over the world every Ford worker carried a copy of

The Flivver King folded in his back pocket sticking out where the boss couldn't fail to see it.

That was quite an ordeal for Henry, I have no doubt. I didn't see him afterwards, and we had no correspondence. He was no letter writer, and I had my say in the book. I told the story of his life, including our meeting, of course, and it was a book that made perfectly plain to the workers the idea that I had tried to make plain to Henry Ford—the idea of democracy in industry. The effect of the whole August strike was that Henry saw he was done for and announced that he was going to close his plants and go out of business. On a certain day, every Ford plant all over the world would close. Well, that of course was a horrible crime and everybody waited with bewilderment and dismay, but when the day came, it didn't happen.

Ford's managers sat down and negotiated deals with the workers' leaders all over the world. I wondered what on earth had done that. Then one day I had an offer for a visit from a man named Sorenson who had been Ford's manager, the one friend that he had in the industry. Sorenson had been Ford's manager from the day that the making of the automobile started. He had run the whole plant and he came to see me and told me the story. He said the reason that Henry Ford gave way was that his wife had told him that if he closed those plants she would leave him and never see him again. That was what broke the proud spirit of the old man. That was what made the old man give way and I never will forget as long as I live the afternoon that I spent in the Ford home with that quiet little woman who sat against the wall and listened. I can't even recall the words she said except a polite welcome and a polite good-bye. But she broke his will. He went back and opened up the plants. They're all running now and the most interesting thing of all is that his grandson is running the plants on an entirely different principle, and he's spending all that Ford fortune on all kinds of useful investigation and discovery. I tell myself that maybe his grandmother taught him something. But anyway those are the stories about the three great families that I reformed in America—the Rockefellers and the Armours and the Fords—and you can all make up your minds whether I'm right or not.